Growing Up with SCIENCE®

Third Edition

11

Plasma physics–Radiotherapy

Marshall Cavendish
Reference
New York

Marshall Cavendish
99 White Plains Road
Tarrytown, NY 10591

www.marshallcavendish.us

Library of Congress Cataloging-in-Publication Data

Growing up with science.— 3rd ed.
   p. cm.
   Includes index.
   Contents: v. 1. Abrasive-Astronomy — v. 2. Atmosphere-Cable television —
v. 3. Cable travel-Cotton — v. 4. Crane-Electricity — v. 5 Electric motor-
Friction — v. 6. Fuel cell-Immune system — v. 7. Induction-Magnetism —
v. 8. Mapmaking-Mining and quarrying — v. 9. Missile and torpedo-Oil
exploration and refining — v. 10. Optics-Plant kingdom — v. 11. Plasma
physics-Radiotherapy — v. 12. Railroad system-Seismology — v. 13.
Semiconductor-Sports — v. 14. Spring-Thermography — v. 15. Thermometer-
Virus, biological — v. 16. Virus, computer-Zoology — v. 17. Index.
   ISBN 0-7614-7505-2 (set)
   ISBN 0-7614-7516-8 (vol. 11)
   1. Science—Encyclopedias.

Q121.G764 2006
503—dc22

2004049962
09 08 07 06 05 6 5 4 3 2 1

Printed in China

CONSULTANT

Donald R. Franceschetti, Ph.D.

Dunavant Professor at the University of Memphis

Donald R. Franceschetti is a member of the American
Chemical Society, the American Physical Society, the
Cognitive Science Society, the History of Science Society,
and the Society for Neuroscience.

CONTRIBUTORS TO VOLUME 11

Tom Jackson

Emma Young

Marshall Cavendish

Editors: Peter Mavrikis and Susan Rescigno

Editorial Director: Paul Bernabeo

Production Manager: Alan Tsai

The Brown Reference Group

Editors: Leon Gray and Simon Hall

Designer: Sarah Williams

Picture Researcher: Helen Simm

Indexer: Kay Ollerenshaw

Illustrators: Darren Awuah and Mark Walker

Managing Editor: Bridget Giles

Art Director: Dave Goodman

CONTENTS

KEY TO COLOR CODING OF ARTICLES

■ EARTH, SPACE, AND ENVIRONMENTAL SCIENCES

■ LIFE SCIENCES AND MEDICINE

■ MATHEMATICS

□ PHYSICS AND CHEMISTRY

■ TECHNOLOGY

■ PEOPLE

Plasma physics

Plasma is the fourth state of matter. Unlike solids, liquids, or gases, it does not consist of atoms or molecules. Instead, plasma consists of a mass of ions and electrons. Plasmas exhibit some of the same physical properties as gases, but, unlike gases, they are good electrical conductors and are also affected by a magnetic field. Plasma may hold the key to Earth's future energy needs.

Matter changes from one state to another state when it is exposed to heat. If a solid is heated above a certain temperature, called the melting point, it becomes a liquid. As more heat is applied, the liquid eventually changes into the gaseous state, at a temperature known as the boiling the point. A plasma can be created by heating a gas to an extremely high temperature. As the temperature increases, the atoms or molecules that make up the gas bump into each other with such force that the electrons are torn away from the nucleus of each atom or molecule and are free to move by themselves. The combination of positive ions and electrons that results is called a plasma.

Physicists have found an easier way to make plasmas. Rather than heat a gas to an extremely high temperature, physicists bombard gases with high-energy electrons. As the high-energy electrons collide with the atoms or molecules of the gas, they knock electrons out of the gas atoms or molecules.

Where plasmas are found

Natural plasmas are rare on Earth. Lightning creates plasma briefly in the air, where the ionized region of air serves as an electrical path for the lightning discharge. The aurora borealis and aurora australis (commonly called the northern and southern lights, respectively) are another example of plasmas in Earth's atmosphere. Auroras are glowing plasmas produced when high-energy

▶ This wide-angle view shows the inside of the torus at the Joint European Torus (JET) laboratory in Culham, Britain. The remote-handling manipulator can be seen to the right of the central column.

▶ *Plasma vapor deposition (PVD) is used to coat a frying pan. The coating, called Cristome, forms a nonstick, scratch-resistant layer on the pan's surface.*

electrons from Earth's upper atmosphere collide with air molecules in the lower layers of the atmosphere, producing a glowing plasma.

Plasma is the most common state of matter in space, making up about 99 percent of the universe. The solar wind is a stream of plasma that radiates from the Sun, and the Van Allen belts are doughnut-shaped regions of plasma that surround Earth in space. Most of the hot matter in the Sun and other stars consists of plasma. There, the plasma takes part in converting matter into energy.

Plasma as an energy source

Teams of physicists from around the world are trying to use plasmas to create energy on Earth. The process involves nuclear fusion reactions between different forms of hydrogen (called isotopes) at extremely high temperatures.

One problem is controlling materials at the high temperatures created during the reactions. The most promising method is to use a device called a tokamak, which is a doughnut-shaped vessel surrounded by magnets. Plasma moves easily along the lines of magnetic fields but is reluctant to move across them. In the early 1990s, important experiments were done using the world's largest tokamaks—the Tokamak Fusion Test Reactor in the United States and the Joint European Torus (JET) in Britain. Scientists at JET managed to produce more than one megawatt of power.

Putting plasma to work

Plasma has other uses. Neon signs are glowing plasmas created by sending a stream of high-energy electrons through a gas-filled tube. Plasma is also used to destroy harmful chemicals. The high temperatures break down complex molecules into simple ones. Plasma is also used to join metals in a process called arc welding. In this process, an electrical current creates an arc—a plasma containing ions of the two metals to be joined. A strong bond forms when the molten metals cool.

See also: FUSION, NUCLEAR • ION AND IONIZATION • LIGHTNING • WELDING

Plastic

Plastics are not found in nature. Most are made out of petrochemicals using a chemical method that joins atoms into long chains. Many everyday items contain plastics. They are also used for specific tasks, such as insulation against heat and electricity. One of the most important properties of plastics is that they can be easily shaped under heat or pressure.

The groundwork for the development of plastics was laid in 1845 by German chemist Christian Friedrich Schönbein (1799–1868) while working in Basle, Switzerland. Schönbein discovered a way to manufacture a compound (chemical combination) of nitrate and cellulose (the substance that makes up the cell walls of plants). Other chemists had tried and failed, but Schönbein's secret was to use both nitric acid (HNO_3) and sulfuric acid (H_2SO_4) with the cellulose, instead of pure nitric acid. When the chemist treated paper with the new compound, the paper became stronger and waterproof. Schönbein could also shape the material easily, and he made several bowls and other items with it. However, he became involved in another project and did not continue his research.

Twenty years later, English chemist Alexander Parkes (1813–1890) invented another material based on cellulose nitrate. Known as Parkesine, it is considered the first commercial plastic. For a time, Parkesine was used for buttons, combs, and knife handles, but it did not become widely popular.

The first successful plastic was celluloid, created by U.S. inventor John Wesley Hyatt (1837–1920) in 1869. Hyatt had entered a contest calling for a material to replace ivory (which was rare and expensive) in the manufacture of billiard balls. He won the $10,000 prize with celluloid—which is cellulose nitrate with the addition of alcohol as a solvent (to make it liquid) and camphor, which imparts thickness and flexibility to the final product. Celluloid was immediately put to many uses, including the manufacture of film, collars and cuffs, and billiard balls.

The main problem with celluloid is that it is extremely flammable. In trying to solve this problem, cellulose acetate was produced by treating the cellulose with acetic acid ($C_2H_4O_2$). This brought its own problem, however, because only poisonous solvents would work on this compound. In 1905, G. W. Miles discovered how to treat cellulose acetate with a mild chemical called acetone (C_3H_6O) as the solvent. This worked well, and the plastic was used as a lacquer for stiffening and waterproofing the wings of aircraft.

Meanwhile, other plastics were also being developed. In 1872, German chemist Adolf von Baeyer (1835–1917) discovered that phenols and aldehydes would produce the kind of materials that could be shaped. U.S. chemist and inventor Leo Hendrik Baekeland (1863–1944) built on this work and, in 1907, he produced a plastic that he called Bakelite. This material became popular during the 1920s, and was used to make many molded articles, such as telephones and electric plugs and sockets.

▶ *Bakelite telephones became popular in the 1920s, with the plastic being ideal as an insulating material for the electrical circuits within the device. Bakelite telephones are now collectors' items.*

▶ *Most polystyrene is produced as solid beads, which are used as protective packaging or to produce molded objects. The foamy structure of polystyrene absorbs shocks well and is very light, so it does not add weight to the packaged articles.*

The work of German chemist Hermann Staudinger (1881–1965) led to the discovery of two important plastics, polystyrene in 1927 and polyvinyl chloride (PVC) in 1933; these are only two of a wide variety of plastics still in use.

How plastics are made

Plastics are made from simple chemicals that form long chains. The starting chemicals (raw materials) are called monomers, and when joined into long chains, they are called polymers. The monomers are forced together by polymerization, which is a method that uses heat and pressure.

Most polymers consist of a chain of carbon and hydrogen atoms because these elements join easily. The monomers needed to make modern plastics are generally taken from petrochemicals. After the pure plastic has been made, it is often improved by adding other materials to give it a different strength, stiffness, or density.

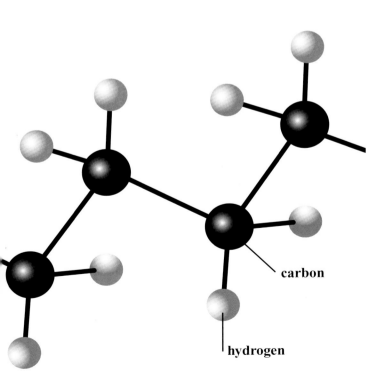

carbon

hydrogen

Modern plastics

Because there are many monomers and different methods of joining them, there are also many different names for plastics. Some plastics, such as Dacron and Formica, are known by their trade names. However, the generic (general) name for most plastics will begin with the prefix *poly-*, for example, polyethylene and polystyrene.

It is easier to study plastics if they are grouped into different "families," some of which are described below. Plastics belonging to the same family often look different, but they all start with the same polymer as their "parent."

Polystyrene

Polystyrene was first made in the 1920s, and new uses are still being found for it. Objects made from polystyrene may be hard (a light switch), or they may be quite soft (a picnic cup or the packaging that holds some toys). The soft type of polystyrene contains many tiny holes that are full of air. This

◀ *This molecular model represents a tiny section of a polyethylene chain. Each sphere represents an atom. The black rods are the bonds between the atoms.*

low-density polystyrene is one of the insulating materials often placed inside cavity walls or the roof of a house to prevent heat from escaping.

The raw materials used to make polystyrene are ethylene (C_2H_4) and benzene (C_6H_6), which are combined to create the monomer styrene. The styrene is then polymerized to make polystyrene.

Polyvinyl chloride

Polyvinyl chloride (PVC) was first produced in the 1930s, but it is still used for many modern items. The starting chemicals are chlorine gas (Cl_2) and ethylene, which react to form vinyl chloride. PVC is the result of polymerizing vinyl chloride.

PVC is often mixed with a substance called a plasticizer, which makes the PVC more flexible. Large plastic sheets used for wrappings and coverings of many kinds are often made from PVC. PVC can also be used to make rigid objects such as drain pipes and gutters on houses.

Polyethylene, polypropylene, and PTFE

Polyethylene and polypropylene belong to the polyolefin family of plastics. By using different temperatures and pressures during the poly-

merization of these plastics, it is possible to change their densities and stiffnesses. These plastics are used for different types of bottles, the wrapping around boxes, water pipes, and many other things.

Another plastic that is related to the same family is polytetrafluoroethylene (PTFE). This is the Teflon coating that is used inside many cooking utensils so that food will not stick to them. The same PTFE can be used as an alternative to grease on metal surfaces because the plastic will prevent the surfaces from sticking or overheating.

Nylons and polyesters

Nylon is a polyamide plastic that was first made in the 1930s. Because it is easily drawn out into thin threads suitable for weaving, stockings and shirts were among the first popular items to be made from this synthetic material. Nylon also can be molded into solid articles, such as gear wheels, which are hard and durable.

Polyester is often known by brand names such as Dacron and Terylene, and it is almost certain to be found in items of clothing. Polyester is often combined with natural textitles, such as cotton or wool, to make fabrics for shirts, dresses, and pants.

◄ *One type of polyester, known as polyethylene terephthalate (PET), is a popular material for making bottles for soft drinks and other forms of food packaging.*

Heating plastics

Most of the plastics described so far are called thermoplastics. If these plastics are gently heated, they will soften, and if they are cooled, they will become hard again. As a result, thermoplastics can be easily shaped by heating.

However, some plastics are thermosetting. Once a thermosetting plastic (like melamine) has been made, it cannot be softened by heating. Thermosetting plastics resist heat, so melamine materials, such as Formica, are used for the tops of kitchen counters. Because this type of plastic is also strong, it is used for the epoxy adhesives (glues).

FORMING PROCESSES

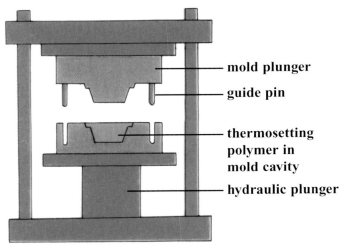

▲ In compression molding, a mold plunger pushes the melted thermosetting polymer into shape (in this example, a bucket). Further heating sets the plastic.

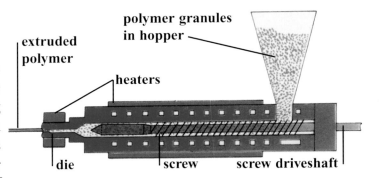

▲ Rods and strips of plastic can be formed by extrusion. Polymer pellets are pushed through a heating chamber by a screw and through an opening of the required shape.

▲ Injection molding is used to make a plastic garbage bin. Injection molding is fully automated and is the most commonly used technique for making thermoplastics such as polyethylene and PVC.

Polyester by itself can also be made into high-quality transparent plastic sheets, such as those used to make photographic film.

Polyurethane

Polyurethane is a widely used plastic that is available in several different forms. Polyurethane foam is soft and flexible, so it is used as stuffing inside chairs and mattresses. Polyurethane foam contains many air pockets, and therefore it is another type of plastic used for insulation, for example, between the inner and outer shell of refrigerators. Polyurethanes are also added to some paints because the plastic hardens the surface of the paint and keeps it from wearing away.

Additives used with plastics

Additives (extra substances) are often added to plastics to make them even more suitable for a particular job. For example, some plastics have a perfume added to improve their aroma. Fillers such as sand, chalk, and sawdust are useful for making plastic more durable. PVC tablecloths contain plasticizer to make them soft, but PVC pipes have no plasticizer in them, and they remain stiff. Plastics are given color by adding dyes or pigments.

Manufacturing with plastics

The great advantage of making things with plastic is that it is easier to shape plastic than such materials as metal or wood. Heating a plastic makes it even easier to press or pull into a new shape.

Items such as buckets and plates are made by a pressure process called compression molding. More complex shapes are made by injection molding in which a hot, soft plastic is injected into a mold that is already made in the shape of the final product. When the plastic has cooled, it is often joined with another shape. On close inspection, you can sometimes see these joints (seams) in an item manufactured from plastics.

> **DID YOU KNOW?**
>
> Polycarbonate is an almost unbreakable plastic that can even stop a bullet. It is used to make reinforced windows and the radioactive core of nuclear reactors.

Long objects without seams, such as pipes, are made by the extrusion process. The softened plastic is extruded (squeezed) through a metal block with openings that force the plastic into shape. Plastic sheets used for making raincoats, tablecloths, and wrappings of various kinds are made by flattening the plastic between hot rollers.

Properties of plastics

Plastic has low density and is therefore useful when a lightweight material is required. The relatively low strength and stiffness of most plastic makes it difficult to use it for construction or for making automobiles. However, by combining plastic with other materials, such as glass fiber, it is possible to make stronger objects, for example, the masts of ships and automobile bumpers.

Even more than metal, heat causes most plastics to expand, and a plastic will usually melt or burn in the case of fire. However, plastics do not pick up and pass on heat, especially if the plastic is foamed and contains many small holes of air. Such plastic becomes insulation when wrapped around pipes or under a roof, keeping the heat inside.

Because electrical current cannot pass easily through plastics, they are often used as electrical insulators. Most of the switches, plugs, sockets, and wires in a house use plastic as the insulator. Cables, pipes, and other objects made out of plastic will usually have a long life because they resist water and weathering better than traditional materials such as metal and wood.

◀ *Some cooking utensils are coated with a plastic called polytetrafluoroethylene (PTFE), better known by the trade name Teflon. The plastic imparts a nonstick, low-friction, and chemically inert lining on cooking utensils such as pans, making them easy to clean.*

▲ *Plastic bottles are recycled into polyester fibers, which resemble natural cotton. Many plastics are not broken down quickly by natural means, so recycling is an environmentally friendly option. However, recycled plastics are of a lower quality than new plastics and cannot be used in applications such as food packaging.*

Special plastics

Composites are products made by mixing plastic with another material, such as glass fiber. Glass reinforced plastic (GRP) is a composite that has been used to make airplane seats and railroad cars. Some objects, such as automobile fenders and surfboards, are made of structural foam, in which softer foamed plastic is protected by a skin of harder plastic. The hard plastic guards against scratches, and the soft plastic inside absorbs energy. Sometimes plastics have been made that combine strength with elasticity. This type of plastic is useful for absorbing vibrations, such as the shaking made by machinery.

Looking to the future

The number of plastics already available is vast, but research in industry and in universities is constantly producing new products. Thousands of new polymers are discovered every year, and many of them will find practical use one day.

New combinations of old plastics are also providing surprising new materials and uses. Future automobiles will have more plastic in their bodies, which are now made of steel, and even in parts of their engines. More plastic will be used in building houses, too. Polyetheretherketone (PEEK) is a new plastic that can withstand high temperatures. It is used to make kettles and the nose cones of aircraft.

See also: CHEMICAL REACTION • FOOD TECHNOLOGY • INSULATOR • POLLUTION • POLYMERIZATION • RECYCLING

Plate tectonics

Earth's crust is broken, like a cracked eggshell, into large sections called plates. These plates are moved around by very strong forces inside Earth. These movements are the cause of many earthquakes, volcanic eruptions, and the formation of mountains. The study of these movements is called plate tectonics.

In the early twentieth century, two scientists—an American named F. B. Taylor (1860–1939) and a German called Alfred Wegener (1880–1930)—independently pointed out that the coastlines of continents on both sides of the Atlantic Ocean had similar shapes. They suggested that North America had once been joined to Europe and that South America had been attached to Africa. The dramatic implication of their suggestion was that the continents must somehow have moved.

Wegener suggested that these continents and other landmasses had all once formed a single landmass—a supercontinent, which he called Pangaea (meaning "all-Earth"). Wegener collected a lot of evidence to support his idea. As well as noting the fit of some of the continents, he found similar rock structures on both sides of the Atlantic, which seemed to have been formed at the same time. He also discovered fossils of the same plants and animals (such as the fern *Glossopteris* and the reptile *Mesosaurus*), dating back about 200 million years, in continents now separated by wide oceans. Wegener also noticed similarities between the ancient climates of some continents. In his book *The Origin of Continents and Oceans* (1915), Wegener claimed that Pangaea started to break up

▼ This map of the world shows the position and movement (shown by the arrows) of tectonic plates. There are three types of plate margins: convergent (thick lines); divergent (thin lines); and conservative (very thin lines). The small orange dots represent volcanoes, which tend to correlate with plate margins.

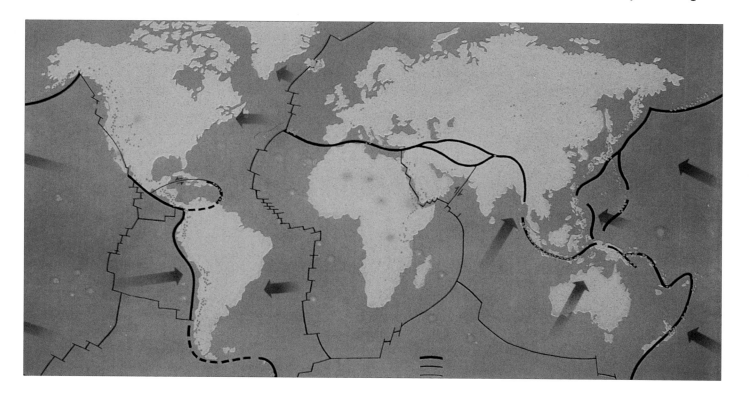

200 million years ago and that the pieces had slowly "drifted" to their present positions. He described this process as continental drift. Wegener could not, however, explain the processes by which huge continents could move.

Convincing the critics

Wegener's theory was so radical that for many years most of the established scientific world was not convinced by it. After World War II (1939–1945), however, two important developments proved crucial in changing scientific opinion: the discovery of paleomagnetism and the development of oceanography.

Paleomagnetism (Earth's magnetic field as it existed in the past) can be established using the principle that in molten igneous rocks (rocks formed by heat) or unlithified sediments (unconsolidated sediment not turned into rock), particles of magnetic minerals, such as magnetite, will align themselves with Earth's magnetic field. This magnetic "record" is stored within igneous rocks as they cool and within sediments when they become lithified. The deviations in the alignment of these paleomagnetic particles from the current direction of Earth's magnetic field show that the continents have moved over time. In the 1930s, English scientist Patrick Blackett (1897–1974) developed a sensitive device called an astatic magnetometer. Using this new equipment, it was possible for the first time to detect the orientation of weak magnetic fields, such as those found in certain types of rock. This allowed researchers to conduct paleomagnetic studies of types of rocks whose magnetism could not be determined using earlier equipment.

Oceanography (the study of the ocean floor) also helped to solve the mystery of continental drift. First, the mapping of the ocean floor showed that around most continents there are gently sloping areas called continental shelves. The edges of the shelves, not the coastlines, are the true edges of the continents. Maps of the continental shelves showed that the edges of the continental shelves fit together like a jigsaw puzzle, even better than the coastlines did.

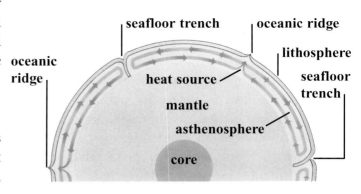

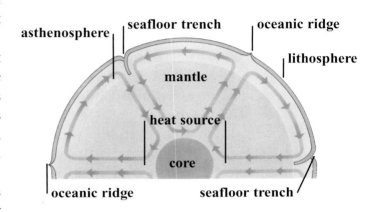

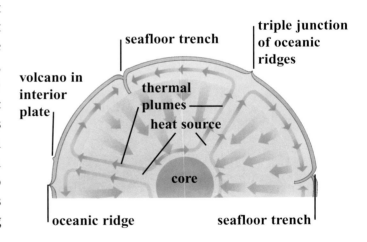

▲ *The illustrations above show three popular hypotheses for the exact mechanism that drives the tectonic plates. Some scientists believe that convection currents are restricted to the top part of the mantle, called the asthenosphere (top). Others think that convection currents flow through the whole mantle (center). Still others believe that tectonic plates are moved by hot plumes of magma, called thermal plumes, which rise to the surface from the boundary between the mantle and the core (bottom).*

There are long mountain ranges called oceanic ridges on the ocean floor. These ridges are areas of earthquakes and volcanic activity. At their centers are the youngest rocks in the oceans—the rocks on the ocean bed get older the farther they are from the ridges in both directions. In fact, most of the rocks on the seabed are less than 200 million years old. Therefore, the oceans are much younger than the continents. Long marine trenches, the deepest parts of the oceans, are also earthquake zones. Alongside these trenches are areas where volcanoes are common.

Plates and plate edges

In the late 1960s, scientists suggested that the oceanic ridges and trenches were breaks in Earth's crust that separated huge, rigid (stiff) plates. They said that these plates were mostly stable—that is, unaffected by volcanoes or even the strongest earthquakes. These plates make up Earth's surface layer, or lithosphere. This rests on, and slides over, a denser, semimolten layer called the asthenosphere. In turn, the asthenosphere surrounds Earth's

> ▼ **Plate tectonics explains how continents are carried along on top of slowly moving plates. It also explains why earthquakes and volcanoes occur.**

DID YOU KNOW?

Earth's lithosphere consists of continental or oceanic crust and an underlying layer of rigid mantle. Continental crust is composed of granitic rocks, which are made up of relatively lightweight minerals such as quartz and feldspar. By contrast, oceanic crust is composed of basaltic rocks, which are much denser and heavier. Since continental crust is much lighter, it floats higher than oceanic crust. Tectonic plates vary in thickness, from about 10 miles (15 kilometers) thick for young oceanic lithosphere, to about 125 miles (200 kilometers) thick for ancient continental lithosphere.

molten inner core. The molten material in Earth's interior is thought to move in convection currents—that is, hot liquid rock rises, spreads sideways, and finally sinks again as it cools. Such molten material is rising underneath the oceanic ridges and spreading out horizontally under the plates. These movements pull the plates apart. The gap created as the plates on both sides of the ridges move is filled with molten material, which hardens

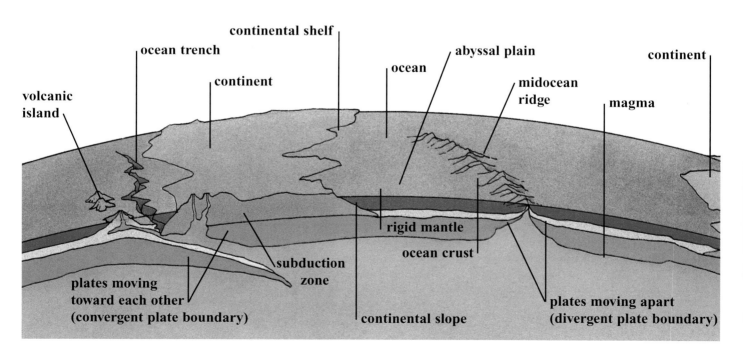

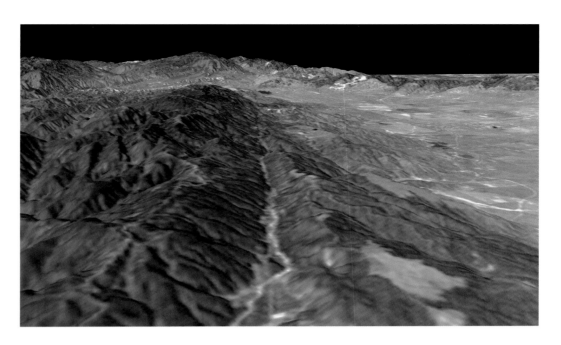

▶ *This true-color radar-generated image shows the Temblor mountain range near Bakersfield, California. The San Andreas Fault is the faint white line to the right of the mountains. To its right is the Carrizo Plain. The San Andreas Fault is the active tectonic boundary between the North American tectonic plate and the Pacific tectonic plate.*

to form new rock. This process is known as ocean spreading, and it forms spreading ridges. These ridges are divergent plate boundaries. The spreading movement along the ridges, which is between ½ and 4 inches (1 to 10 centimeters) each year, is not smooth. The Mid-Atlantic Ridge, which splits nearly the entire Atlantic Ocean north to south, is probably the best-known example of a divergent plate boundary.

While new rock is forming along the oceanic ridges, other rock is also being destroyed. In these areas, called convergent plate boundaries, two plates push toward each other. Cooling molten rock in the convection currents start to sink back into the mantle. As a result of convergence, one plate is pushed under the other, forming deep trenches. This area is called a subduction zone. As the plate descends in a series of jerks, which cause earthquakes, it melts. The magma (molten rock) formed in this way often rises under pressure and is forced into mountain ranges in Earth's crust. A good example of a convergent plate boundary is the Peru-Chile Trench off the coast of South America. There, the dense oceanic Nazca Plate is pushing into and being subducted under the lighter continental crust at the South American Plate boundary. In turn, the overriding South American Plate is being lifted up, creating the Andes Mountains.

Converging plates can eventually jam together in collision zones. Downward movements of advancing plates stop, and rock and sediments are squeezed together to form high mountains. The collision between the Indian and Eurasian plates, for example, has pushed up the Himalayas and the Tibetan Plateau.

A plate edge that can be seen on Earth's surface is the transform fault. Such faults are huge fractures (breaks) or a series of fractures where two plates are moving alongside each other. Such movements are usually jerky, because the rough edges of the plates become jammed together. Eventually the pressure becomes stronger, the jam breaks, and the plates lurch forward, causing earthquakes. The best-known fault of this type in the United States is the San Andreas Fault, which marks the meeting of the Pacific Plate and the North American Plate. Starting at the Gulf of California, the fault extends northwesterly for about 650 miles (1046 kilometers) and passes into the sea north of San Francisco. Movements of the two plates along this fault have caused many earthquakes, such as that of 1906, which destroyed much of San Francisco.

See also: EARTH • EARTHQUAKE • MOUNTAIN • VOLCANO

Platinum group metals

In order of atomic number, the platinum group metals are ruthenium, rhodium, palladium, osmium, iridium, and platinum. This group of dense, silvery-white transition metals is rare and, therefore, the metals are very expensive. However, they have many uses, ranging from catalysts and spark plugs to coinage and jewelry.

During the Spanish conquest of the Americas, Spanish explorers discovered an unknown metal while searching for gold and silver. The explorers called the new metal *platina del Pinto,* which means "little silver of the Pinto River." They gave it this name because they discovered a large quantity of platinum in the Pinto River in Colombia. The Spanish explorers took samples back to Europe. When chemists analyzed the samples, they realized that the substance was a completely new metal. However, the discovery went largely unnoticed for the next two hundred years.

In 1735, Spanish scientist Antonio de Ulloa (1716–1795) was traveling in South America when he rediscovered the metal. He returned to Spain with more samples, and this time the discovery caused much interest. When French chemist François Chabaneau (1754–1842) found a way of purifying the metal, platinum became popular as a decorative metal for jewelry. By the end of the nineteenth century, the metal was in great demand.

The platinum samples discovered in South America were actually a mixture of platinum and palladium. In 1802, British scientist William Wollaston (1766–1828) isolated palladium from the waste products left behind after he had purified a sample of platinum. Two years later, Wollaston discovered rhodium. Around the same time, another British chemist, Smithson Tennant (1761–1815), discovered iridium and osmium. The last platinum group metal, ruthenium, was isolated in 1844. Swedish chemist Jöns Jakob Berzelius (1779–1848) and German chemist Gottfried Osann (1797–1866) isolated ruthenium oxide from a sample of platinum, but they could not extract the metal from its oxide. They gave a sample of

▶ *Ingots and nuggets of pure platinum metal shine with a silvery white luster. Platinum retains its luster because it resists attack by moisture and oxygen in the air.*

▶ *Froth flotation is one of the ways used to separate platinum from its ores. First, the mineral-rich rock is crushed and mixed with water and various chemicals. Air is then pumped through the mineral mixture, and the bubbles created carry the mineral particles to the surface, which is skimmed off.*

ruthenium oxide to Russian chemist Karl Karlovich Klaus (1796–1864), who successfully isolated the pure metal in 1844.

Separating the metals

Platinum is a rare metal. It is sometimes found in its native state, which means the metal is not mixed with any other substances. Native deposits are found in Colombia and in the Ural Mountains of Russia. Pure platinum is also mined in South Africa and Canada. In South Africa and the United States, platinum is also found in ores—platinum compounds locked inside rocks. Some common platinum ores are sperrylite (platinum arsenide; $PtAs_2$) and cooperite (platinum sulfide; PtS). Platinum is also found mixed with other platinum group metals. Separating the platinum group metals from each other is very difficult.

First, a mixture of platinum group metals is placed in a hot solution of aqua regia, which is a mixture of three parts concentrated hydrochloric acid (HCl) to one part concentrated nitric acid (HNO_3). The aqua regia dissolves the platinum and palladium, and they are filtered from the solution, purified, and burned to produce the pure metals. The part of the mixture that does not dissolve in aqua regia is reacted with molten sodium chloride (NaCl) at 1292°F (700°C). This separates out the ruthenium, rhodium, and iridium, leaving osmium behind in the sludge.

Platinum group catalysts

The platinum group metals are very useful catalysts (substances that help speed up chemical reactions), and so they are often used as pollution-control devices in automobile exhaust systems. The

▲ *Rhodium–platinum bushings are used to produce glass fibers by drawing molten glass through the holes.*

DID YOU KNOW?

The platinum group metals have many important applications in medicine. For example, platinum-iridium alloys are used to make surgical instruments and medical implants. Platinum group metals are useful for this purpose because they are inert metals and therefore do not react with the tissues and fluids inside the body. They are also good electrical conductors, so they are ideal materials for the electrodes for devices such as pacemakers and aural and retinal implants. Platinum is also important as a drug in the form of the compounds cisplatin and carboplatin. Drugs containing these compounds are used to treat ovarian and testicular cancers. The compounds work by stopping the cancer cells from dividing, limiting the spread of the cancer cells to other areas of the body.

catalysts convert harmful chemicals from burned gasoline, such as carbon monoxide and nitrogen oxides, into harmless nitrogen gas, carbon dioxide, and water vapor. Platinum group metal catalysts play an important role in the production of many different acids. Nitric acid is made by passing a mixture of ammonia gas (NH_3) and oxygen gas (O2) over a hot gauze made of a mixture of platinum and rhodium. The gases first form an intermediary compound, called nitric oxide (NO), which is then converted into nitrogen dioxide (NO_2). The nitrogen dioxide then dissolves in water to form nitric acid. Palladium has also replaced nickel as the catalyst used in margarine production. The palladium is crushed into a very fine powder, called a black, which can spread over a greater area and work better and faster.

Platinum group alloys

All the platinum group metals have extremely high melting points, so they are often used to make items that must withstand very high temperatures, such as the components of jet engines and spacecraft. For example, platinum is used to make the radio antennas on space vehicles. The reflectors in the

Many people think that gold dulls and yellows the appearance of diamonds in jewelry. Since platinum retains the natural brilliance of a diamond, it is often used as the setting for the gem in engagement rings.

antennas consist of more than one hundred platinum wires. The reflectors beam radio signals sent from the satellite back to Earth.

Another property of the platinum group metals is that they do not react easily with other substances. As a result, scientists sometimes use a small vessel, called a crucible, made from platinum group metals to contain samples that must be heated to very high temperatures.

While pure platinum group metals are often used for these purposes, sometimes it is best to use alloys. Alloys are mixtures of two or more metals, or a metal and a nonmetal such as carbon. Alloys containing platinum group metals have many useful applications. For example, they are used to plate the switch contacts in electrical equipment. Fountain pen points are usually made from alloys of iridium, osmium, and platinum because the alloys are not corroded by the chemical action of the ink in the pen. In automobiles, the same alloys are used in the electronics that control engines and in the mechanism that triggers airbags. Since they resist spark and heat damage, the tips of

automobile spark plugs also consist of platinum group alloys. An alloy of iridium and platinum is used to make a high-temperature thermometer called a thermocouple. Thermocouples produce electrical signals that change as the temperature of the substance being measured changes. Factories making materials such as steel use these devices to monitor the temperatures of the molten products.

Decorative metals

Platinum and palladium are often used in jewelry as the settings for precious gemstones. Since they are both very soft when they are pure, platinum and palladium are usually alloyed with rhodium to make them stronger. Some of the biggest and most expensive diamonds in the world are set in platinum. An example is the Koh-i-noor diamond, which is owned by the British monarchy and is set in a crown made of pure platinum metal.

See also: ALLOY • CATALYST • ELECTRONICS • METAL • TRANSITION ELEMENT

Plow

The plow is an agricultural tool used to break up and turn over the top layer of soil in fields. Simple wooden plows were used long before the days of the ancient Roman Empire. The modern plow is still a very important tool to the farmers of today.

The plow is designed to soften, break up, and turn over the top layer of soil in fields to make them ready for planting crops. The plow cuts narrow grooves, called furrows, in the soil. The cutting action also breaks the soil up into smaller lumps. It also allows the air and winter frost to help break down the clods of mud still further. Turning the soil over also helps bury any weeds that may be growing on the surface. There they decompose and release much-needed nutrients back into the soil.

How the plow works

A simple plow consists of a fixed iron knife blade, called a coulter, that cuts a vertical slit in the soil. Behind this is a plowshare, which is another blade of a different shape. The plowshare cuts the furrow horizontally underneath the vertical slit. A curved metal plate, called moldboard, turns over the soil from the furrow.

The history and development of the plow

The first plow dates back to the Stone Age. It was a simple forked branch tied to a pole. The two ends of the branch were the handles, and the part below the fork was the plowshare. The pole was used to pull the plow, and it was probably dragged by people at first. However, it was not long before animals, such as cattle, mules, and oxen, were used to make the job much easier.

The Mesopotamians were skilled farmers. They replaced the forked branch with wooden shafts set in a wooden block. Another of their improvements

▲ *This plow is being pulled by oxen and is guided by the farmer, who follows on foot. Animals continue to provide the pulling power for plows used in agriculture in the developing world.*

made it possible to sow and plow at the same time. This was done by drilling a vertical hole in the block and fixing a tube with a funnel top into it. The seeds could be poured through the funnel while the farmer plowed the field.

By about 4000 years ago, a different kind of plow had come into use in Europe. It was also a forked branch, but one arm was cut short and sharpened to form the plowshare. The other arm was left long to serve as the pulling pole. A single handle left one hand free to guide the ox team.

Since the soil in much of Europe is heavy and damp, the plowshare would skid over the surface. This problem was solved by fixing a sharp blade, called a coulter, to the pole, just ahead of the plowshare. The coulter opened up the soil so that the plowshare could cut into it more easily.

The moldboard was added to turn the soil over as well as dig it. The moldboard slips under the slice of soil cut by the plowshare and forces that slice over. There were two important results of this invention.

It could work land that had been too hard to plow before, and it could make channels in the hills so that rainwater would drain away. However, the greater weight of the moldboard made the plow heavier and more difficult to use. The light, easily worked soils of the Mediterranean lands did not need such an advanced and heavy plow.

Developing the modern plow

The plow stayed much the same until the eighteenth century, when it was made lighter, and some changes were made to the frame. The coulter and plowshare were specially shaped to cut a furrow of a particular shape. The moldboard was also changed so that it first lifted and then slowly turned the sliced earth over.

With the discoveries and improvements of the Industrial Revolution, iron began to replace wood as the material of choice for tools such as plows. In 1803, British inventor Robert Ransome (1753–1830) patented the hardening process that allowed iron to be made self-sharpening. U.S. blacksmith John Deere (1804–1886) introduced the first steel plow in the 1830s. Deere's invention opened up the prairies of the Midwest to the pioneers, who began to farm the land.

During the second half of the nineteenth century, the steam plow became popular. This plow was drawn across a field by cables attached to a static engine. Several plows could be used at the same time, but the system was expensive to repair.

An important development in 1936 was a mechanism that connected a plow to a tractor. Today, most farmers in the developed world plow their land with rows of plows on wheels. They are pulled across the fields behind tractors.

Modern plows

Where the soil is dry and hard or sticky, the disk plow works much better than a plow with a moldboard. The disk plow has one or more deeply cupped disks set at an angle in the plow frame. A furrow slice is cut and pushed aside by each disk.

In temperate climates, where land is neither sticky nor too dry, the moldboard plow is still widely used. Most plows with moldboards cut three furrows at a time, although some can cut up to ten furrows. Furrows are cut between 10 and 16 inches (25 and 40 centimeters) wide. The depth of the furrow is about half the width, although heavy soils are usually plowed much deeper.

A less common type of plow is the chisel plow. It breaks up the soil without turning it over and is used for plowing cereal stubble.

There are two methods of plowing for both moldboard and disk plows—fixed and reversible. Fixed plowing requires dividing up the field so that individual sections can be plowed separately. This leaves ridges between the sections. Reversible plowing leaves a more even surface.

◄ *A modern plow is connected directly to the back of a tractor. The resistance of the soil on the plow acts as a downward force on the tractor, making it more stable. Hydraulic arms powered by the tractor's engine keep the plow level and control the depth of plowing.*

See also: AGRICULTURE

Pluto

Pluto is one of the most unusual planets known in the solar system. Two-thirds the size of Earth's Moon, but 12,000 times farther away, Pluto is neither like any of the inner, rocky planets, such as Earth, nor like the outer, gaseous planets, such as Jupiter.

In the early twentieth century, astronomers noticed that something appeared to be disturbing the orbits of Uranus and Neptune—the outermost of the eight planets known in the solar system at the time. These astronomers believed that a mysterious "Planet X" existed farther out in the solar system and was gravitationally disturbing the orbits of Uranus and Neptune. It was as a result of a detailed search for Planet X that Pluto was discovered in 1930 by U.S. astronomer Clyde Tombaugh (1906–1997), who was working at Lowell Observatory in Flagstaff, Arizona.

Pluto, however, is such a small planet that astronomers realized it could not be responsible for the disturbances of the outer planets, as they had imagined. Pluto's discovery was therefore a fortunate accident.

Studying Pluto

From Earth, Pluto is visible through only the most powerful telescopes, and then only as a small point of light that resembles a very faint star. Pluto's motion through space is very slow because of its great distance from the Sun, but it can be seen to change its position slightly night by night.

Pluto's brightness varies by about 12 percent over 6.387 Earth days. This variation in brightness indicates that some areas of the planet's surface reflect much more light than others and that Pluto makes one complete rotation every 6.387 days.

The best images of Pluto are from the Hubble Space Telescope and the Infrared Astronomical Satellite. These imaging devices are placed in space and thus are unaffected by the distortions caused to land-based equipment by Earth's atmosphere.

Pluto's orbit

Pluto is so far away that it takes 248 Earth years to orbit the Sun. At its farthest point, Pluto lies nearly 4.6 billion miles (7.4 billion kilometers) away from the Sun. Its closest point is about 2.8 billion miles (4.5 billion kilometers) away. Most of the time, Pluto is the farthest planet from the Sun, although one of Pluto's many oddities is that for 20 years of its 248-year orbit, it travels inside the orbit of the eighth planet, Neptune.

◀ *This photograph of Clyde Tombaugh was taken shortly after his discovery of Pluto in 1930. Tombaugh made several other important discoveries during his career, including six star clusters, one cloud of galaxies, one comet, and about 775 asteroids.*

DISCOVERY OF THE PLANET PLUTO

January 23, 1930

January 29, 1930

These are copies of small sections of the discovery plates showing images (those marked) of Lowell's mathematically predicted trans-Neptunian planet afterward named PLUTO. It was found by Mr. C. W. Tombaugh on February 18, 1930, while engaged in the search program and upon examination of these plates.

Lowell Observatory Photograph

▲ *These photographs are the first evidence of Pluto. In the left image, the arrow marks an unknown body. The image on the right shows the object's position six days later. This movement was a sign that this was a planet.*

Other oddities of Pluto include the shape of its orbit, which is very elongated (stretched). Also, Pluto's orbital plane (the angle of its orbit) is at a very different angle from the orbital planes of the other planets. Pluto's axis (the imaginary line around which it rotates) is unusual, being tipped about 122 degrees relative to its orbital plane. Like Uranus, Pluto lies nearly on its side. Last, Pluto rotates in retrograde motion—that is, in the opposite direction to most of the other planets.

DID YOU KNOW?

Astronomers have been studying Pluto since its discovery in 1930 but still know very little about it. Because of Pluto's great distance, observation from Earth is very difficult, even with powerful telescopes. The most significant observations have been made with the Hubble Space Telescope and the Infrared Astronomical Satellite, both of which orbit Earth above its atmosphere. No spacecraft has visited Pluto, although such missions are now being considered.

Pluto's physical characteristics

For many years it was thought that Pluto was larger than the planet Mercury. However, recent studies have shown that it can be no bigger than about 1,440 miles (2,320 kilometers) across. This makes Pluto by far the smallest planet in the solar system. Its diameter is less than half that of Mercury, and several moons, including Earth's, are larger.

The overall color of Pluto is thought to be slightly reddish, with brighter ice caps at the poles. The composition of the planet is unusual. It was once thought that Pluto might be a heavy, rocky body like Earth. Now it is thought that Pluto is a very light body, mostly comprising rock and also ice. Pluto's density has been estimated at about 110 pounds per cubic foot (1,750 kilograms per cubic meter), which is less than a third that of Earth. This density indicates that the planet is probably a mixture of about 70 percent rock and 30 percent ice.

Early infrared measurements, made in the 1970s, revealed the presence of methane ice (CH_4) on Pluto's surface. Later scientific instruments have revealed the presence of frozen nitrogen gas (N_2) in the largest quantities, as well as amounts of frozen carbon monoxide (CO) and ethane (C_2H_5). These surface ices are thought to be responsible for the high reflectivity of much of Pluto's surface. The composition of the darker areas of Pluto's surface is unknown, but they may be due to silicates, ancient organic compounds, or photochemical reactions driven by cosmic rays.

Astronomers think that Pluto does not have an atmosphere for most of the time. For the majority of Pluto's long year (248 Earth years), all gases are probably frozen into ice. When Pluto is closest to the Sun, however, there may be enough heating for sublimation to occur (the frozen gas sublimes, which means it turns directly from a solid to a vapor). The planet may then have a thin gaseous atmosphere, probably consisting primarily of nitrogen, with some carbon monoxide, methane, and ethane. The surface temperature of Pluto is estimated to lie between 40 Kelvin (–233°C or 388°F) and 50 Kelvin (–223°C or –370°F). Astronomers estimate that at its farthest distance from the Sun the surface temperature may drop into the teens on the Kelvin scale.

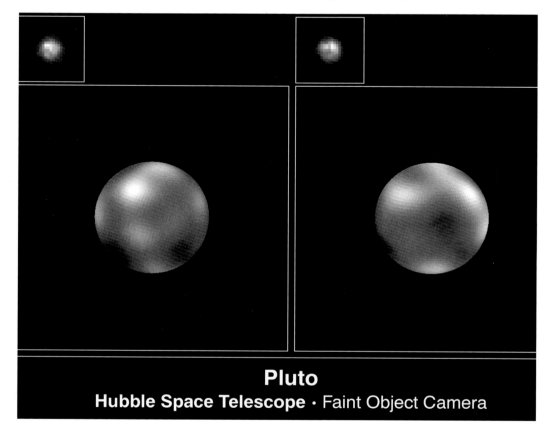

Pluto
Hubble Space Telescope · Faint Object Camera

◄ *These computer-enhanced images of Pluto were taken by the Hubble Space Telescope. The images, which show both sides of the planet, show that Pluto is an unusually complex object. Pluto has more large-scale contrast than any planet, except Earth. The two inset pictures are the actual Hubble images from which the computer enhancements were made.*

▲ *This artist's impression shows the* **New Horizons** *spacecraft during a planned encounter with Pluto and Charon. Due to be launched in 2006,* **New Horizons** *would reach Pluto by 2015. The craft's science equipment is designed to analyze the landscapes and geologies of Pluto and Charon and map their surface compositions and temperatures.*

Charon

In 1978, U.S. astronomer James Christy, working at the U.S. Naval Observatory, discovered that Pluto had a moon. Christy called this moon Charon. Charon is about one-third the size of Pluto, with a diameter of about 790 miles (1,270 kilometers). Charon orbits Pluto in a little over six hours. This is the same time it takes for the planet itself to rotate on its axis, so from Pluto, Charon would always appear to be in the same place in the sky. Pluto is the only planet to have a natural satellite in a synchronous orbit like this.

Charon has a slightly lower reflectivity than Pluto and is more neutral in color. Little is known about its composition, but a low density, similar to that of Pluto, suggests that it, too, does not contain a high percentage of rock. Water ice is thought to be present. Charon most likely lacks any atmosphere.

Classifying Pluto

Since Pluto is very small and has an unusual composition, some astronomers now believe that Pluto should not be considered a true planet. Instead, it is suggested that Pluto should be classed as a minor planet, or planetoid. Others have even suggested that Pluto is not a planet at all, but the largest member of the Kuiper belt, a region of small, icy cometlike bodies beyond Neptune.

See also: ASTRONOMY • SOLAR SYSTEM

Poison

A poison is a substance that can damage the normal function of the body. Poisons can enter the body through the skin, mouth, or lungs. Many household products contain poisons, including cleaning products such as bleach and even medicines. Insect stings, industrial chemicals, and cigarette smoke also contain dangerous poisons. All these things are common, so it is easy to forget how dangerous they can be.

▼ *Venom is extracted from a puff adder at the School of Tropical Medicine in Liverpool, Britain. Venom is a poison that snakes inject into their prey through fangs (teeth). This venom either kills or immobilizes the prey.*

Every day, thousands of people are admitted to the emergency room because they have been poisoned. Most people come into contact with poisons accidentally, either around the house or at school or work. Some people take poisonous substances deliberately, often as a cry for help because they are depressed, and sometimes because they feel that they cannot go on living. Most of these cases could be prevented if dangerous substances were not readily available.

What is a poison?

It is difficult to explain exactly why some substances are poisonous and some are not. Even drinking vast amounts of water can be dangerous; and many useful medicines, such as aspirin, can be poisonous if too much is taken within a certain period of time. A poison is therefore any substance

▶ *This Vietnamese child was born with twisted arms and legs in a maternity hospital in Ho Chi Minh City, Vietnam. Her deformities are a result of her parents' exposure to Agent Orange, which was used to remove unwanted plant life that provided cover for enemy forces during the Vietnam War (1954–1975).*

that, in large quantities, can harm the body. Obvious poisons are some industrial chemicals and toxic gases and fumes. For example, automobile exhaust fumes contain two types of poison. Carbon monoxide (CO) is very dangerous. Inhaling just a small amount of carbon monoxide causes people to lose consciousness. Inhaling too much will lead to death. For this reason, an automobile should never be left running in an enclosed space, such as a garage. Exhaust fumes may also contain small amounts of lead. In large amounts, lead is very harmful, especially to the brain.

Less obvious poisons are contained within everyday household chemicals such as bleach, disinfectants, paints, and polishes. Even food can cause poisoning if it has not been cooked or stored properly. Many plants, such as foxglove and poison ivy, contain poisons, and animals, such as some insects, snakes, and spiders, have a poisonous bite.

How does a poison work?

Some poisons work in an obvious way. Corrosive substances, such as acids, burn the skin, so they will burn the mouth and stomach if they are swallowed. Most poisons are more complex. Taking too many sleeping tablets, for example, affects the brain so that it no longer controls breathing. Starved of oxygen, the major organs shut down, resulting in death. Other drugs, such as antidepressants, can damage the heart. When taken in large amounts, acetaminophen has no harmful effect at first. Inside the body, however, it is changed into a poison that damages the liver. Fortunately, liver damage can be prevented if treatment is given within 24 hours.

Symptoms of poisoning

Poisons can cause sleepiness, unconsciousness, or pain, but the most noticeable symptom of poisoning is sickness and vomiting. This is usually

DID YOU KNOW?

Most snakes only bite people when they feel frightened or threatened. When the snake bites, it injects its venom into the body through or near its fangs. General symptoms of snake bites include swelling and extreme pain, followed by nausea, numbness, and lethargy. Within a few hours, convulsions and respiratory and renal failure may follow. Fatal poisoning from snake venom is rare in the developed world, however, because hospitals keep stocks of "antivenins" to treat the effects of particularly dangerous snake venoms.

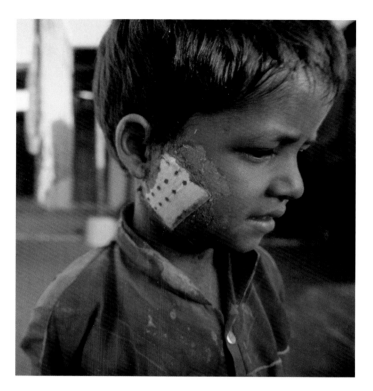

◄ *An injured child attends a protest for the treatment of victims of the Union Carbide disaster in Bhopal, India. The factory was the site of a poison gas leak in December 1984 that claimed thousands of lives and injured tens of thousands of other inhabitants.*

due to burning and irritation of the stomach lining, but sometimes it is because the poison has affected the part of the brain that controls vomiting. Some painkillers cause no symptoms at all.

Methanol, which is found in solvents and antifreeze, can cause blindness. Inside the body, it changes into substances that damage the nerves leading to the eyes. Petroleum compounds cause little damage to the stomach or intestines, but they can be very harmful if they get into the lungs.

Treatment for poisoning

Anyone suffering from poisoning should be taken to see a doctor at the hospital emergency room, even if there are no obvious symptoms. If possible, it is important to bring along some of the tablets or poisonous substance so that the doctor can see what has been taken and will know immediately the type of treatment to give.

The treatment given for poisoning depends not only on what poison has been taken but also the amount that has been consumed. Sometimes the person is made to vomit so that the poison is removed from the body. Alternatively, the stomach may be washed out using warm water poured down a tube. Some poisons can be washed out of the bloodstream using an artificial kidney machine. Sometimes a drug called an antidote can be given to overcome the harmful effects of the poison. In many cases, however, the body deals with the poison in its own way, and all that the person needs is to be watched carefully by medical professionals until the period of danger has passed.

After a case of poisoning, there are usually no aftereffects. If a strong, burning poison such as an acid or bleach has been swallowed, however, the doctor may want to determine if the way in which the person swallows has been affected. If a large amount of acetaminophen has been taken, it is important to ensure that the liver has not been permanently damaged. The person will be admitted to the hospital and monitored for a few days.

Who can be poisoned?

Obviously, there is a possibility of accidental poisoning at any time in a person's life, but there are times when the risks are greater than usual.

Babies are most at risk because they naturally put things into their mouths, especially liquids and brightly colored objects such as some pills or

▲ *Cigarette smoke is one of the most common toxic air pollutants. It contains more than 4,500 carcinogenic (cancer-causing substances), including arsenic, benzene, formaldehyde, and hydrogen cyanide.*

tablets. Some young people feel that they have problems with which they cannot cope, for example, the stress of exams or problems with their parents or peers. Some may attempt suicide by taking too many painkillers or other medicines. In most cases, the intention is simply to attract attention to the problem. However, death may be the unfortunate consequence because of the powerful effects of the substances they have taken. Adults may also try to poison themselves if they feel depressed or suffer from a painful terminal illness. Poisoning in these cases is often fatal.

Preventing accidental poisoning

The most dangerous substances in the home are usually found under the kitchen sink, in the bathroom cabinet, in the basement, and in the garage. Cupboards containing poisonous substances must be locked, so the substances are kept out of reach of children. Medicines should be stored in childproof containers, and any unused medicines should be safely discarded. Some medicines may look like candy, but they can be very dangerous.

Wash your hands immediately after handling any poisonous substance, and wash out any containers such as cans and buckets, being careful not to leave them in the kitchen or near food.

DID YOU KNOW?

Fugu is a Japanese fish stew that contains the meat of the puffer fish. However, the intestines of these fish contain a powerful poison called tetrodotoxin, which is not destroyed during the cooking process. Japanese chefs must hold a license to prepare this dangerous delicacy, since expert preparation is vital.

See also: BRAIN • DRUG INDUSTRY

Polarization

Sometimes, when a person looks at an object in a very bright light, he or she cannot see it easily because of the glare of natural light. This glare can be cut down using a polarizer, such as Polaroid sunglasses. The polarizer cuts out some of the light and makes it easier for people to see.

Ordinary light is produced by the electrons in a hot object, such as the Sun or a lightbulb, moving around in all directions. This sort of light is called unpolarized, because the light waves vibrate in all directions. However, light can be split into two separate beams so that in each beam all the light waves vibrate in the same direction. These beams of light are said to be polarized. The light waves in one beam vibrate vertically, and in the other beam the light waves vibrate horizontally.

Making polarized light

Polarized light is normally produced by splitting up ordinary unpolarized light into two polarized beams and then eliminating one of them. Lasers can be made to produce polarized light, because the slanted ends of the laser tube can eliminate one of the beams by reflecting it away. This leaves only the other beam of light, in which all of the light waves are vibrating in the same direction.

Different types of polarizers

Most modern polarizers are made from a kind of plastic that allows one polarized beam of light to pass through but absorbs the other beam. These are called dichroic polarizers. Dichroic polarizers, such as Polaroid, can be made cheaply in large sheets. Some crystals, such as tourmaline, are also dichroic but are more expensive than plastic polarizers.

U.S. inventor Edwin Herbert Land (1909–1991) developed his plastic sheet polarizer in the late 1920s while studying at Harvard University. Land

◀ *Polaroid sunglasses are very good at cutting out the glare of natural light, making it easier for people to see. The plastic lenses of the glasses let through only vertically polarized light, so the glare is reduced.*

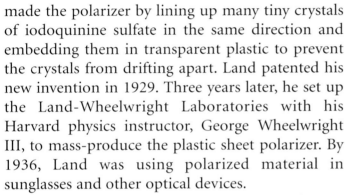

▲ *These two photographs were taken by the same camera. The photograph on the left was taken through a polarizer, while the photograph on the right was taken in ordinary unpolarized light. The polarizer cuts down the glare of natural light.*

made the polarizer by lining up many tiny crystals of iodoquinine sulfate in the same direction and embedding them in transparent plastic to prevent the crystals from drifting apart. Land patented his new invention in 1929. Three years later, he set up the Land-Wheelwright Laboratories with his Harvard physics instructor, George Wheelwright III, to mass-produce the plastic sheet polarizer. By 1936, Land was using polarized material in sunglasses and other optical devices.

Before Land invented his plastic sheet polarizer, people often used a Nicol prism to polarize light. The prism takes its name from its inventor, Scottish physicist William Nicol (1768–1851). Nicol took a crystal of Iceland spar (calcium carbonate; $CaCO_3$), cut the crystal in half, and then cemented the crystal together again with a type of resin called Canada balsam. The crystal was shaped in such a way that one of the light beams was reflected completely inside the crystal. The other beam, though, was able to pass straight through. The Nicol prism made a huge impact on the study of chemistry, because it could be used to measure the angle of polarization of different compounds.

Sending signals

When television signals are transmitted from a television station, they are polarized. People need an antenna that can receive polarized signals to watch television at home. Some stations send signals that are horizontally polarized, while others send signals that are vertically polarized. When signals sent on the same frequency are polarized in different directions, they do not interfere with each other.

Checking and measuring

Polarized light can be used to test parts before they are put into machines. First, a copy of the part is made in a transparent (see-through) plastic, such as Bakelite. The plastic part is placed between two polarizers, and white light is shone onto it. When the part is put under stress by being twisted or pushed, the white light is broken up into colors that show where the stress is greatest and where the part is likely to break first.

Polarized light is often used to measure how concentrated a solution is. If a polarized beam of light is shone onto a sugar solution, the sugar molecules can turn the light so that it shines in a different direction. By measuring how far the light beam has moved around, the strength of the solution can be determined.

See also: ANTENNA • LIGHT • TELEVISION

Pollution

Pollution is the spoiling of the land, air, or water by artificial waste products. It is often a nuisance, and sometimes it is a threat to people's health. The rapid growth of population, cities, and industry continue to make pollution a worldwide problem.

Pollution comes in many forms. Generally, pollution is considered to be the waste materials that are produced by factories, engines, and by other human activities. These wastes are released into the air, into rivers and the ocean, or are buried on land. Waste often contains poisons, and if it is not managed properly, it may pollute the environment and damage communities of wildlife and even affect human health.

However, there are other types of pollution. An airport or busy highway produces sound pollution. The loud noises produced by airplanes, trucks, and automobiles interferes with the rest of the surrounding environment. Street lamps that light up cities at night also produce light pollution. The lamps are meant to light up the ground, but they also often light up the night's sky. This gives the sky an orange glow that confuses wildlife, such as birds, which think it is still dusk or already dawn. The light also blocks out the fainter starlight. The land can be polluted in other ways as well. For example, open-pit mining, quarrying, building new roads, electricity pylons, and advertising billboards can spoil beautiful scenery.

Waste materials and pesticides

Modern civilizations produce huge amounts of waste. On average, every person in the United States produces 56 tons (50 tonnes) of waste every year. This includes everything from sewage to unwanted automobiles. Many waste materials are broken down by bacteria into harmless substances. These

▲ Pollution has a damaging effect on wildlife. Large amounts of pollution may kill all the animals in the area, but smaller amounts of pollution may gradually reduce the amount of wildlife in an area until little or no plants or animals remain.

things are said to be biodegradable. However, other substances, including plastics, do not break down, and they stay in the ground or ocean for years.

Farmers also pollute the land, often by mistake. For example, they may spray crops with pesticides that kill insects. The poisoned insects are eaten by small animals and birds, and these, in turn, are eaten by larger hunters, such as birds of prey. This interaction is called the food chain, and the pesticide can pass along it. At each stage in the chain, the poison becomes more concentrated in the tissues of the animals. Generally, pesticides are completely harmless to large animals. In the past, however, more damaging substances have been used that killed wildlife or made it hard for them to breed.

One pesticide, dichlorodiphenyltrichloroethane (DDT), was developed in 1940. It killed many kinds of insects, and it was valuable in controlling insects that spread diseases, such as malaria. However, DDT does not break down naturally after it has been sprayed. As a result, DDT has spread widely from the areas where it was first used. It has even been found in the Arctic and Antarctic oceans.

Also, many insects became resistant to DDT, and larger amounts were needed to do the same job. However, the chemical built up in the bodies of the insects before it killed them. When these insects were eaten, the DDT was carried up the food chain. At the top of this food chain were birds of prey and other hunting birds. The DDT did not kill these animals, but it made the shells of the eggs they laid very thin. The eggs often smashed in the nest before the chicks could hatch, and the numbers of hunting birds, such as cormorants, bald eagles, and pelicans,

went down very quickly. Many almost became extinct. By the 1970s, DDT was banned in most developed countries.

Pesticides are now designed to break down into harmless substances quickly, and they are just as effective as more long-lasting chemicals. Often the pesticides are so effective that they kill all of the insects in an area. Unfortunately, this leaves no food for the insect-eating birds and mammals.

Water pollution

Water may be polluted in several ways. For example, hot water, even if it is clean, can upset the balance of nature in rivers and lakes.

Another source of water pollution is untreated sewage, which is still pumped directly into many waterways. Oxygen is needed for sewage to break down. Hence, if too much sewage is pumped into slow-flowing rivers or lakes, the oxygen in the water is soon used up. Plants and animals, including the small creatures that break down the sewage, die. This process is called eutrophication. The lifeless waterway becomes a source of disease because there is no oxygen to help break down the raw sewage. A similar effect occurs when fertilizers, such as nitrates and phosphates, are washed from farmland

◄ *Even useful substances, such as fertilizers, can cause pollution. If fertilizer gets into water, it causes the microscopic algae in the water to grow quickly. This creates a bloom of thick green sludge on the surface of the water, causing problems for animals that live in the water.*

into water. The fertilizers are added to soils to make crops grow faster. If they end up in rivers, they also make the water plants grow quickly. The plants form a green sludge on the water's surface and use up all the oxygen.

Factory waste

Industrial wastes are sometimes pumped directly into waterways in many areas, poisoning the organisms that live in the water. Through natural food chains, the poisons build up in fishes and shellfish that people eat. In many parts of the world, people are now advised not to eat too much shellfish caught in many coastal waters or fish caught from certain waterways.

The danger of pollution of coastal waters was shown in the early 1950s. A chemical company was pumping industrial wastes into Minamata Bay, on the west coast of the Japanese island of Kyushu. The

families of fishermen, who lived on the fish and shellfish from the bay, started to become sick from an unpleasant but unknown illness, which later became known as Minamata disease. Sufferers had mental problems, became deaf and blind, and felt very tired. Over the next few years, hundreds of fisherman died.

It was eventually discovered that the people were being poisoned by mercury in the waste produced by the chemical plant. This poison was taken in by the marine animals, which were then eaten by the fishermen's families. Perhaps as many as ten thousand people were affected by this poisoning. It took 40 years for the amount of mercury in the bay to return to safe levels.

Oil spills

Oil is another pollutant that comes from factories and empties into rivers and lakes. Some rivers contain so much oil that they are fire hazards. The Cuyahoga River in Ohio once caught fire.

Oil pollution in the open sea has a terrible effect on sea creatures, including seabirds and animals that live on polluted coastlines. The causes of oil slicks (large areas of floating oil) include accidents on oil tankers or blowouts at oil rigs. The largest oil spill in U.S. history was in Alaska's Prince William Sound in 1989. The Exxon tanker *Valdez* ran aground on rocks and spilled nearly 11 million gallons (41 million liters) of oil.

Oil and other pollutants are especially dangerous in enclosed or nearly enclosed seas, such as the Mediterranean Sea and the North American Great Lakes. These bodies of water do not have large tides to mix up the water and wash away pollution and garbage. Some of the Great Lakes, such as Lake Erie, are so polluted that they virtually have no animal life left in certain places. Perhaps the most polluted sea is the Aral Sea, a once large inland sea on the border of Kazakhstan and Uzbekistan in Central

◄ *Oil and water do not mix, and when petroleum is spilled into the ocean, it floats on the surface of the water. Any seabirds that land on the water become coated with oil. This damages their feathers and makes the birds too heavy to fly and feed.*

▲ *Air pollution, especially from automobiles and other road vehicles, creates smog during certain weather conditions. Smog is fog mixed with smoke. It hangs over crowded cities, such as Mexico City pictured above, for several days and can cause breathing problems for many people.*

Asia. Over the last 50 years, the sea has shrunk to half its size. The river water that fills the sea has been diverted onto fields for irrigating crops. The area surrounding the sea is now a polluted desert. The sea's water is three times as salty as it was in the 1960s, and it also contains a lot of industrial pollution and fertilizers.

Air pollution

Smoke, soot, and gases poured into the air by factories and homes burning fossil fuels can cause unpleasant smog. Smog is a word meaning "smoky fog." It is a thick mixture of smoke and moisture in the air that makes it difficult to see and breathe. The particles of moisture often contain acids, which corrode (eat away) stonework and metals. Smog is

also a health hazard. In the 1950s, for example, it was once a regular winter problem in London and other English cities. The British government passed a Clean Air Act in 1956, forcing factories and homes to use smokeless fuels. Smoke was greatly reduced, and smog is no longer such a problem.

Automobiles and trucks are now responsible for about half of all air pollution. They release the poisonous gas carbon monoxide (CO), unburned hydrocarbons, oxides of nitrogen, and smoke particles. Sunlight reacts with the particles to form photochemical smog. Many cities have smog problems caused by the exhaust from cars. Mexico City, Jakarta (Indonesia), Athens (Greece), and Los Angeles are especially hard hit.

Smog problems are worse during weather conditions called temperature inversions. These occur when air near the ground is colder and heavier than warmer air above it. The cold air, which is filled with pollution, cannot rise above the warm air, so it stays trapped close to the ground until the temperature changes and the air can escape.

The United States has introduced laws to reduce pollution by exhaust fumes. All cars are fitted with catalytic converters, which convert the pollution into less harmful emissions, such as water and carbon dioxide (CO_2).

Acid rain

The rain that falls from the sky is not pure water. It normally contains other chemicals, such as carbon dioxide dissolved from the air. This makes rain a weak carbonic acid (H_2CO_3). However, sulfur dioxide (SO_2) and nitrogen oxides released into the air also dissolve in rain. This makes rain contain stronger acids called sulfurous acid (H_2SO_3) and nitric acid (HNO_3). This acid rain has damaged lakes and forests across the world. Only a few plants like an acidic environment, and acid rain makes it hard for other plants to extract the nutrients they need from the soil. Without enough plants to eat, forest animals are also affected.

◄ *This forest has been damaged by acid rain. Acid rain contains sulfurous acid, which is produced when sulfur dioxide gas mixes with rain water. The sulfur dioxide is released when certain fuels, such as coal and gasoline, are burned.*

In the 1980s, acid rain was threatening many parts of North America and northern Europe. The lakes and forests, especially in Canada and Scandinavia, were becoming badly damaged by air pollution, which was often being produced in other countries. The worst pollution came from coal-burning power stations in countries such as Germany, Britain, Japan, and the United States. Chemical scrubbers were installed in any chimneys that were releasing sulfur dioxide or nitrogen oxides. These scrubbers worked a little like the catalytic converters in automobiles and removed the acid-causing chemicals.

Acid rain is less problematic in North America and western Europe. However, certain areas of eastern Europe and Asia are still badly affected by acid rain. Even tropical rain forests are suffering from acid rainstorms.

Pollution and climate change

The atmosphere is mainly nitrogen and oxygen gas. It also contains small amounts of carbon dioxide, water vapor, and other gases.

Most living things need to take in oxygen to survive. They then release carbon dioxide as a waste product. However, green plants also take in the carbon dioxide and combine it with water to make sugars. This is how they make their food and consequently how they grow.

Fossil fuels such as natural gas, coal, and gasoline are formed from the remains of plants that grew millions of years ago. The plants were buried, and the carbon they contained was trapped deep underground. When fossil fuels are recovered and then burned, the carbon dioxide that has been locked inside them for millions of years is released into the atmosphere again. Over the last two centuries, people have burned so much fossil fuels that the amount of carbon dioxide in the atmosphere has increased.

▲ *During the Persian Gulf War in 1991, Iraqi forces set on fire many of the oil wells in the deserts of Kuwait. This created huge amounts of smoke and other air pollution, which turned the sky black for months. Burning oil and other fossil fuels is the main cause of global warming.*

This change is having an effect on the world's climate. Carbon dioxide (along with other gases) in the air traps heat in the atmosphere. Light from the Sun passes through the air and warms Earth's surface. Earth then releases this heat, but some of it is trapped by the carbon dioxide. The whole world has been getting warmer very slowly. The gases in the air work in the same way as glass does in keeping a greenhouse warm. Carbon dioxide and other gases, such as methane, are thus called "greenhouse" gases. Scientists are not sure what the effects of Earth's warming will be. However, it is very likely that as the world's oceans warm up, the

water will expand and take up more room. This will cause sea levels to rise, and many coastal regions will be flooded. It is very hard to predict by how much the sea level will rise, but it is likely to be several feet over the next century if nothing is done.

Although many places will enjoy warmer weather if global warming continues, some will actually get colder, and other places will turn into deserts. Weather patterns are also being altered by global warming. The land warms up more quickly than the oceans, and in a warmer world, the difference between the two is becoming greater. This larger difference in temperatures produces more storms and other violent weather.

Global warming can only be slowed if people release less carbon dioxide into the air. They can do this by using energy more efficiently and by not burning as much gasoline or other fuels. Another way is to use sources of power that do not release

◄ *Tall chimneys, or superstacks, are used to release pollution high in the sky so they do not affect people on the ground. However, the pollution generally returns to the ground as acid rain.*

carbon dioxide. At the moment, nuclear power is the only method of producing electricity in large amounts without releasing greenhouse gases. However, nuclear power plants produce a lot of other very dangerous pollutants.

In the future, people may be able to harness the power of the wind, tides, and Sun to power machines and heat homes. These sources of energy produce no pollution, but they are still too inefficient to provide all the energy people need.

Nuclear waste

The waste products of nuclear power are the most long-lasting types of pollution humans produce. Nuclear power plants use nuclear fuel, such as uranium, to produce heat. The heat is then used to make electricity. The atoms in the fuel release heat by splitting apart into smaller atoms. This process

releases dangerous radiation, so nuclear reactors must be well shielded. When a certain fraction of the atoms in a fuel element have decayed, the build up of waste products makes the fuel no longer suitable for reactor use, even though it is still dangerously radioactive. It will take hundreds of thousands of years for radioactivity of the spent fuel to reach a safe level.

Nuclear power plants produce three types of waste. Low-level waste includes materials such as the protective clothing worn by plant workers and other contaminated equipment, such as glassware and pipes. Radioactive materials are used in hospitals and laboratories. The equipment used to handle them is classed as low-level waste. Intermediate-level waste is the material used during the reprocessing of nuclear fuel. This involves extracting any useful materials left behind after fuel has been used in a nuclear power plant. High-level waste is the product of reprocessing.

All nuclear waste must be stored safely for a long time. Some high-level wastes will be unsafe for nearly half a million years. All high-level nuclear waste is currently stored in temporary sites. Soon, however, it will be moved to underground storage sites where it can be left until it is safe. Engineers have never had to build anything that will last this long before. Most storage sites will be designed to work safely for only about ten or twenty thousand years. At some point in the distant future, the waste will probably have to be checked and moved to another site. A high-level storage site is currently being developed inside Yucca Mountain in Nevada. Before the waste is buried, it will be made as safe as possible by turning it into glass or ceramic.

Toxic waste

Companies that produce dangerous waste must make it safe before they release it into the environment. It is against the law not to do this. It is the job of the U.S. Environmental Protection Agency (EPA) to check that toxic waste and other pollution does not get into the water, air, and soil.

Dangerous waste must be disposed of carefully. Simply burying the waste is not a good method of disposal. For example, during the 1940s and 1950s, chemical waste was dumped at Love Canal in New York State. Later, the burial site was covered with clay to try to keep the poisons in the ground. Eventually, homes were built on the land. Some time afterward, smelly sludge began to appear in the basements of the houses. It was discovered that dangerous chemicals were present. Investigators also found that people living in the area suffered from poor health, and many children were born with deformities because of the buried waste.

▲ *A scientist measures pollution in a lake using an electronic chemical analyzer. Scientists can also see the effects of pollution on an area by surveying how well certain plants and animals are growing.*

Disposing of waste

Liquid waste can be made safe by mixing it with other chemicals before it leaves the factory. If this is not possible, a process called biological oxidation is often used. The liquid wastes are allowed to trickle down through beds of gravel and sand. Millions of bacteria in the sand and gravel use oxygen to convert the toxic chemicals into safe products. Some industrial waste is so toxic that it would kill the bacteria. These are often burned.

Burying wastes

Other industrial wastes are buried, although many may need to be processed biologically beforehand. Unlike the old dumping sites, modern landfill sites are strictly controlled. They are chosen because they are not affected by earthquakes or volcanos. It is also important that the buried waste does not leak into water in the ground. The EPA issues licenses for these sights, which give permission to bury only certain chemicals.

At one huge landfill site in Essex, England, about 1,000 tons (980 tonnes) of household garbage arrive each day from London. This forms the base material into which 700 tons (635 tonnes) of liquid industrial waste are mixed each day. The liquid and solid wastes are treated chemically and biologically. Eventually, safe solids are buried, and the safe liquids are pumped out to sea.

Incineration

Toxic wastes cannot be broken down biologically, or they take too long to decompose into safe products. They are often disposed of by incineration (high-temperature burning). This is carried out in complex furnaces that operate at temperatures of over 2000°F (1100°C). The gases produced by the furnaces are cleaned by being passed through chemical scrubbers before they are released into the air. Incineration is the best way of destroying the most dangerous chemicals.

See also: ACID AND ALKALI • GLOBAL WARMING • NUCLEAR REACTOR • RADIOACTIVITY

Polymerization

Polymerization is a chemical process in which many small molecules link up to form very large molecules called polymers. Natural polymers include asbestos, hair, rubber, and starch. Nylon and various kinds of plastics are synthetic polymers.

The word *polymer* comes from the Greek words *poly,* which means "many," and *meros,* which means "a part." The word is a good description of a polymer, because each polymer molecule consists of a chain or network of thousands of single repeated molecules, called monomers. A polymer may consist of as many as 100,000 monomer units. Natural polymers, which are found in both animals and plants, include cellulose, proteins, and starch. Synthetic polymers include artificial resins, nylon, and many different types of plastics.

If a polymerization involves molecules of just one chemical compound, the result is called a homopolymer, from the Greek word *homo,* which means "same." If two different monomers are involved, the product is called a copolymer. Chemists have also been able to mix several polymers together after polymerization to produce a new polymer, called a polymer blend.

Polymerization reactions

A polymerization reaction is a chemical reaction in which a polymer is formed from monomer units. There are three main polymerization reactions.

The most important process is called direct polymerization. In polymerization reactions, a single chemical compound or two closely related compounds react with each other. For this to happen, the monomer must have more than one chemical bond. Ethylene is a good example because it has a double bond between the carbon atoms:

$$CH_2=CH_2$$

When the monomers react to form the polymer, the double bonds between the carbon atoms split apart. They form two single bonds that link the monomer molecules together in a polymer chain called polyethylene. Polymers can also be made from compounds similar to ethylene. The polymer polystyrene is made from the styrene monomer, $CH_2=CHC_6H_5$, while polyvinyl chloride (PVC) is made from the vinyl chloride monomer, $CH_2=CHCl$. Both styrene and vinyl chloride have the same carbon double bond as ethylene.

◄ *The cotton-ball part of the cotton plant contains a lot of cellulose. Cellulose is a natural polymer made up of long chains of glucose molecules.*

The other two important polymerization mechanisms are condensation and addition. Both involve two different monomers reacting to form the polymer. Condensation polymerization takes place when the two monomers react to produce the polymer molecule accompanied by the loss of a molecule of ammonia (NH_3) or water (H_2O). Nylon, polyester, and various other polymers are produced through condensation polymerization. In addition polymerization, the monomers are dissolved in a solvent, and they quickly combine without losing any atoms. The resulting polymer therefore has the same basic chemical formula as the monomers from which it is made. The solvent is then removed.

How polymerization works

There are three stages involved in a direct polymerization reaction. To start the reaction there must be chain initiation. The monomer has to be activated so that its molecules can bind together. For chain initiation to begin, the monomer

▲ *Agricultural workers cover strawberry plants with long sheets of the plastic polymer polyethylene. The plastic cover traps heat, retains moisture, and protects the delicate crops from the cold at night.*

DID YOU KNOW?

U.S. chemist Wallace Hume Carothers (1896–1937) and his team of researchers at E. I. du Pont de Nemours & Company developed nylon during the 1930s. Carothers was studying the structure of long-chain molecules formed by joining different atoms. In 1930, he chanced upon a substance that formed strong, flexible fibers. Recognizing the potential of this discovery, Carothers and his team of organic chemists looked for a way of making the fiber on a commercial scale. By 1938, they had succeeded. The new fiber, called nylon, paved the way for the synthetic fiber industry.

molecules must be activated by applying pressure, by heating, by shaking or stirring, or by adding chemicals, called catalysts, that start the process.

Once the monomer molecules are activated and start to react, they link up to form the chains or networks of molecules that form the polymer. This stage is called chain growth. In chain growth, an activated molecule joins to an unactivated molecule and forms a new activated molecule that consists of two monomer molecules. This new activated molecule then reacts with another unactivated monomer molecule to give an activated polymer molecule of three monomer molecules. The process will continue to repeat itself until the activated polymer molecule consists of many thousands of monomer molecules, all joined together. This growth can be stopped only by deactivating the polymer chain, usually with another activated monomer molecule.

If **M** is an unactivated monomer molecule and **M*** an activated monomer molecule, this is a brief outline of the mechanism of the polymerization:

Activation	$M \rightarrow M^*$
Growth	$M^* + M \rightarrow M–M^*$
Growth	$M–M^* + M \rightarrow M–M–M^*$
Termination	$M–M–M^* + M^* \rightarrow M–M–M–M$

Polymerization processes

When polymers are made in industry, a number of different processes can be used to make the process as efficient as possible. Bulk polymerization is a

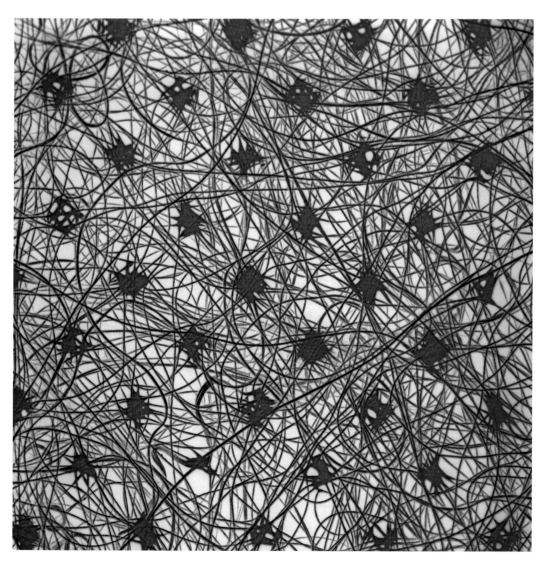

◀ *This color scanning electron micrograph (SEM) shows filaments of the plastic polypropylene, which is formed by the polymerization of propylene. Polypropylene is similar to polyethylene, but it is stronger, lighter, and more rigid. It is also a thermoplastic, which means that it can be repeatedly softened by heating and hardened by cooling. Polypropylene is used to make various solid products and fibrous materials.*

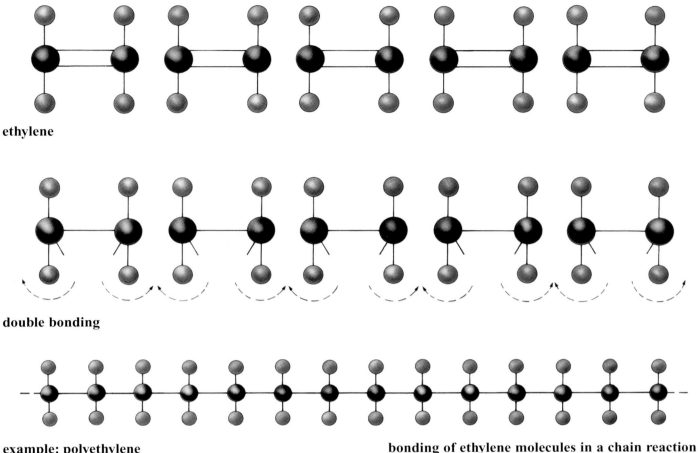

ethylene

double bonding

example: polyethylene

bonding of ethylene molecules in a chain reaction

⬤ **carbon**   ⬤ **hydrogen**

▲ *Polyethylene is made by linking together ethylene molecules. The double carbon bonds in each molecule are opened to link the molecules together.*

continuous process. The monomers are placed in a container where they polymerize directly. The temperature of the reaction needs to be carefully controlled as it produces a lot of heat.

In emulsion polymerization, the monomers are added to water, where they break up into tiny droplets about ¹⁄₂₅,₀₀₀ inch (1 micron) wide and form what is known as an emulsion. The emulsion is heated to a temperature of between 160 and 210°F (70 and 100°C). A polymerization catalyst that dissolves in water is then added. The monomer droplets then polymerize into solid polymer particles and the water is removed.

In suspension polymerization, the monomers are stirred with water to form droplets of between ¹⁄₂₅ and ³⁄₅₀ inch (0.2 to 1.5 millimeters) across. A

polymerization catalyst that dissolves in the monomer is then added. The liquid monomer droplets then polymerize to form solid beads. These are then separated from the water and dried.

Polymerization depends on the temperature and pressure of the reaction container, the number of monomers present, and many other factors. By changing these factors, different polymers can be produced from the same monomers. When catalysts are used to initiate polymerization reactions, they often determine structural properties that have important effects on the chemistry of the polymer.

See also: CHEMICAL REACTION • PLASTIC • PROTEIN

Population growth

Despite wars and continued famine, the number of people living in the world is growing every day. Increased medical knowledge and improved living conditions are probably the main reasons for this population explosion.

Thousands of years ago, life was very dangerous. Herbal medicines were all that people had to treat the sick. The dangers were many—eating poisonous berries or drinking polluted water, being bitten by snakes or mauled by wild animals, accidents such as drowning or falling, wounds from tribal wars, and disease and lack of food. As a result of all these problems, the number of people surviving childhood and then living into old age was fairly low.

People are intelligent and inventive, however, and over time, solutions to these problems were found. As conditions improved, the human population grew until it has reached such proportions that it has been called a population explosion.

Settlements and progress

Gradually, the early hunter-gatherers found pleasant and suitable sites to set up permanent camps. These early settlers began to plant crops and keep animals that could provide food. They learned to improve their seeds and animals through careful selection and breeding. This gave them better harvests and hardier animals that could survive through bad conditions. If they could grow more

▼ *This overcrowded refugee camp in Kibumba, Zaire, is testament to the world's population explosion. It is often difficult for people to settle in new areas when they are displaced from their native land.*

food than they needed for themselves, they were able to trade the excess for goods they could not produce or for services none of the people in the settlement could provide. This specialization of work other than farming was important to the growth of civilization.

Little by little, life became less hazardous. Knowledge and learning increased, and ideas were exchanged. Scientific and medical discoveries had a huge impact on the kind of life and the age to which most people could expect to live.

Where on Earth?

All the continents (except Antarctica) are thought to have been populated ten thousand years ago. With a total population of only about five million, however, the people were scattered very thinly around the world.

▼ *This portrait shows three generations from the same family—grandchildren, parents, and grandparents. Increased longevity and a reduction in infant mortality have led to a marked growth in the world population.*

Around 70 percent of Earth's surface area is covered with water. Of the remaining 30 percent of Earth's surface area, only 10 percent is considered to be habitable (fit to be lived in). The rest consists of frozen waste, deserts, and tropical forests. The inhabited part of Earth is called the ecumene, and the rest is called the nonecumene. Throughout human history, the ecumene has been getting bigger, particularly during the last two hundred years. Even so, at the beginning of the twenty-first century, about half the world's four billion people lived on about 5 percent of the world's land.

The world's population is distributed very unevenly over Earth's surface. The density of a population can only give a sketchy idea of the spread or distribution of people because it assumes that they are evenly scattered through a region or country and, of course, that is not the case. Rather, there are clusters of people; for example, there's a cluster in South and Southeast Asia, another cluster in East Asia, a third in eastern North America, and a fourth in Europe. Two more clusters are in

DID YOU KNOW?

There are various highly effective methods of avoiding pregnancy. These include barrier methods, such as condoms, diaphragms, and caps. Male condoms are worn over the penis and prevent sperm from entering the vagina. Female condoms, diaphragms, and caps fit inside the vagina and cover the cervix to prevent sperm from reaching an egg. Intrauterine methods involve the insertion of a small device into the uterus. Contraceptive pills work by preventing the ovaries from releasing an egg each month. New methods of contraception include the introduction of hormone implants that offer protection against pregnancy for several years.

industrial areas of Asia, for example, in Japan, Hong Kong, and Taiwan. Unlike the other clusters in Asia, where life is poorer and is based on a rural economy, people generally enjoy a good standard of living in these areas. The populations of industrialized countries are usually to be found mostly in the cities and towns.

Coping with the numbers

The continued increase in world population is controlled by the rate at which birthrates rise and death rates fall. During the nineteenth century,

▼ *A woman uses a dispensing machine to obtain free contraception. The machine was installed in a suburb of Beijing, China, as part of a pilot project for family planning and AIDS prevention. China has passed family-planning laws that advocate delaying marriage and child bearing and limiting the number of children to one child per couple.*

▲ *These children are living in a refugee camp in Angola. Their distended stomachs are a symptom of severe malnutrition, which is a major cause of childhood death in the developing world.*

populations grew most quickly in Europe and those countries to which European immigrants moved, such as Australia, Canada, and the United States. The rise in the European population was mainly due to better living standards and improvements in sanitation and medicine, which meant that the death rate fell. However, this fall in the death rate was offset by the decline in the birthrate that occurred in some Western countries.

DID YOU KNOW?

In 2004, there were an estimated 6.4 billion people living on Earth. The United Nations (UN) estimates that the world's population in 2050 will range between 9.3 billion to a possible high of 10.9 billion.

In the less-developed countries, medical progress in the twentieth century brought about a rapid fall in the death rate, and especially in infant mortality since World War II (1939–1945). As a result, a greater number of women survived to childbearing age, and so there was an increase in the birthrate and survival of the resultant offspring. Sadly, the population explosion was fastest in those countries least able to support the extra people.

Feeding the extra people can be done by bringing new land under cultivation, for example, by irrigating dry lands. Furthermore, rich and fertile nations can export their extra food in exchange for manufactured goods and services from countries rich, perhaps, in minerals. This requires a lot of planning and cooperation, so an international alliance to alleviate hunger has been proposed by the United Nations.

See also: DISEASE • MEDICAL TECHNOLOGY • PREGNANCY AND BIRTH

Pottery

From the very earliest times, people throughout the world have made pots, bowls, and other items for everyday use from baked clay. This craft is called pottery. In fact, making pottery is one of the oldest and most widespread of all the arts.

At different times, people in many parts of the world discovered that clay could be molded and then baked into very hard objects. This is pottery—the making of pots. Many other clay objects from the distant past have been discovered buried in the ground. These show the amazing skill of ancient peoples, who could create beautiful and useful forms, colors, and decorations in pottery.

The oldest pots were shaped in two ways. One was to press a slab of clay over a gourd (a squash-like plant). This gave the pot a rounded bottom that would not stand upright. The other was to roll out many small coils of clay and place them in layers to build up the sides of a pot.

Pottery was dried in the air to help keep the clay from cracking during the firing, and then it was placed in a small fire to harden it. This process is still called firing. To stop the finished pot from soaking up water, the surface was rubbed smooth with a pebble while the clay was still damp. This closed up any tiny holes in the surface. It also gave the surface a shine after firing.

About ten thousand years ago, people began using an oven, called a kiln, to fire pottery. At first, a fire was lit below a clay shelf, which held the pots. Later, a low wall was built up around this shelf to hold in the heat better. Then the wall was built

higher so more shelves and thus more pots could fit. Finally, the kiln wall formed an enclosed dome with several shelves inside. The kiln was hotter than an open fire, and it also kept pots out of the flames. Previously, the flames had spoiled the decorations on the pots as they were being fired.

People began to decorate the surface of their pots with colored slips. Slip is a thin mixture of clay and water. It could be colored with powdered rocks or with the juices of vegetables.

The shaping of pots also improved as people began to use the potters wheel. This device is a wooden turntable that spins around while the potter works on a single lump of clay thrown in the center. The ancient Egyptians were using the potters wheel at least six thousand years ago.

Two thousand years ago, the Romans began to produce a lot of pottery by pressing the clay into molds instead of making each piece on a wheel.

▶ *This amphora (storage jar) was made near Athens, Greece, about 2,500 years ago. Archaeologists know how old it is by the way it is designed and painted. They use amphoras and other old pieces of pottery to figure out the age of the other remains that they find.*

Shiny surface

The glaze is a liquid that is applied to a pot before firing. After firing, the glazed pot is less porous, shinier, and can also be colored. A greenish blue glaze was used in ancient Egypt and Mesopotamia about 1,700 years ago. It consisted of finely ground white sand mixed with sodium carbonate (Na_2CO_3), which gave the pottery a hard, glassy coating. In the second century BCE, the Chinese and the Romans used lead oxide (PbO_2) as a glaze. The Chinese green glaze of that period is especially famous. By the early tenth century CE, China had discovered the art of making porcelain, which is a thin, white, and very light pottery. This became quite popular, and even now porcelain is often referred to as china.

China clay

China clay (kaolin) is a fine white clay that is used to make china. Kaolin was named for the mountain in northern China where the clay was mined for hundreds of years.

China clay was being used in China earlier than three thousand years ago. China pots were first brought to Europe by Portuguese explorers about four hundred years ago. Kaolin was later found to exist in Europe itself. The first china clay mine in Europe was in Cornwall, England.

In modern times, about half the kaolin produced is used to make glossy paper. Kaolin is also used for filling rubber to increase its strength and in paints, inks, and some cosmetics.

How china clay is formed

China clay is a soft, white mineral deposit that consists of a mineral called kaolinite, which is made from the elements aluminum, silicon, and oxygen. China clay forms over many thousands of years from a group of rock-forming minerals called feldspars. These minerals turn into clay by reacting with acids underground.

Small deposits are found in most countries, but large workable deposits occur only in the southern United States and in Britain, China, the Czech Republic, France, Germany, Russia, and Spain.

▲ *A potter throws a vase on a potter's wheel. Early pottery was made by hand in this way. The spinning creates a force inside the clay that pushes it out to the edges of the wheel, making it easier for the potter to form a circular object. The potter pushes into the center of the clay to make it hollow. The clay must be kept wet to stop it from breaking apart and to make it easier to mold into shapes.*

Mechanical diggers remove the topsoil to get at the clay underneath. Then the clay is washed by high-pressure water hoses. The resulting mixture of clay, water, and other minerals is pumped to a sand separation plant. There, the coarse quartz sand is removed and carried to the top of the sandpiles that can be seen wherever there are clay works.

Ceramics

The best known use for china clay is for making ceramic objects used in homes and by industry. To start, the clay is mixed with water in a tank called a

▲ *Filter presses squeeze the water out of china clay to make flat sheets called filter cakes. These are firm enough to handle but still flexible enough to mold.*

blunger. The slip is then pumped into a vat called an ark with other ingredients that depend on what type of china is being made. For example, bone china, which is light, contains 25 percent clay, 25 percent powdered stone, and 50 percent bone ash.

The next stage is to turn the liquid into a form that can be easily molded. Most of the water is squeezed out by filter presses, which produce flat sheets called filter cakes. These are then put into pug mills, which remove the remaining water and air bubbles, producing a cylinder of clay.

Molding is now done by machines rather than the slow potter's wheel. For example, to make a plate, a slice is cut from the cylinder of clay, put onto the bottom half of a mold, and pressed into shape by a rotating press. Cups are made by forcing a lump of clay against the side of a cup-shaped mold with a rotating tapered roller.

For a difficult shape, such as a teapot, a technique called slip casting is used. A plaster mold is prepared and cut in half lengthwise; the halves are joined again, and the slip is poured into the mold. As the plaster of the mold begins to absorb the water, the slip at the side begins to thicken, and a thin wall of dry clay is formed. After a time, the excess slip inside the clay wall is poured out, and the mold is put in the drying oven. When dried, the mold is opened up, and the unfired pot is removed. Then it is glazed and fired. Basins, sinks, and toilets are also made by slip casting.

The pottery is fired in a kiln. The firing process vitrifies the clay, which means that the outside become hard and glasslike. It also seals the pot so it does not absorb the liquids that are poured into it.

A modern kiln is usually a tunnel up to 100 yards (92 meters) long, in which the temperature is hottest in the middle. The article of pottery is put on a kiln car, which is drawn slowly through the tunnel. The hardening process, vitrification, needs a temperature of about 2192°F (1200°C), and the firing cycle takes between 14 and 30 hours. What comes out of this first firing is strong, white chinaware. It is now ready for decoration and glaze.

Porcelain

Museums often have ancient Chinese vases and bowls on display. These articles are made of porcelain, and they are considered works of art. People still think of porcelain as valuable and beautiful, so it is used to make expensive tableware.

Porcelain is a hard, white pottery that has a beauty because it is translucent—that is, light shows through it. Porcelain is also very durable and does not absorb water or let it leak out. For these reasons, people like to eat and drink from porcelain tableware. However, the Chinese inventors of porcelain did not make it for tableware. This use began in Europe in the eighteenth century.

The history of porcelain dates back to 1028 BCE, when the Chinese discovered how to produce a more translucent pottery than their traditional stoneware. Their success was achieved partly because they had such good raw materials with which to work.

Chinese porcelain is made from kaolin and petunste, which is a kind of granite made of feldspar and quartz minerals. These substances produce what is called hard paste porcelain. It must be fired at very high temperatures.

By the third century CE, the Chinese had learned how to fire their pottery at 2282°F (1250°C). By the tenth century, they were making fine pottery similar to modern porcelain. During the years 960 to 1279, under the Sung Dynasty, the Chinese brought the manufacture of porcelain to a high art. The quality dropped, however, when Chinese craftspeople started to export china to Europe in the eighteenth century.

The finest porcelain is first fired at temperatures of 1652 to 1832°F (900 to 1000°C) and a second time at 2563 to 2684°F (1350 to 1400°C). Before the second firing, it is glazed. The kaolin holds the shape of the object, and the petunste vitrifies it. It is this glassy finish that makes porcelain so highly prized. However, one of the problems with all pottery, especially porcelain, is that once vitrified it becomes very brittle. Brittle objects shatter easily. The very high temperatures in the kiln also may make some of the pots shatter as they are fired.

Chinese porcelain spread into Europe by way of the sea trade in the late seventeenth century. China objects were very expensive in Europe and the United States because they had to be transported by sea from East Asia. Soon, Europeans were trying to produce their own. The first success did not come until 1710, when German chemist Johann Friedrich Böttger (1682–1719) was experimenting in Meissen, Germany. He discovered a way to make porcelain with local clay and minerals, and this was the start of the famous Meissen china industry.

In England, the first China porcelain was made by William Cookworthy (1705–1780) in Cornwall. His factory operated there from 1768 to 1770.

All this time, porcelain was developing along another line. Arabs had also learned about porcelain through their trade with China and had begun to produce it themselves. Of course, they did not have the same kind of clay or minerals, so the type of porcelain they developed is called soft paste. It cannot be fired at such high temperatures as Chinese, or hard paste, porcelains and therefore it is not as strong. On the other hand, it is less expensive to produce because it requires less heat. Lower temperatures in the kiln also mean that less pots are broken while being fired.

Arabs brought their porcelain technology with them as the moved across North Africa, conquering new territory. Arabs also introduced it to southern Spain when they ruled that region. From Spain, it spread across Europe, especially to Italy. The first Italian porcelain from Florence was made of clay and frit (ground glass). The first firing temperature was 2012 to 2192°F (1100 to 1200°C) and the second was lower—1922°F (1050°C).

In England, William Duesbury (1735–1802) and Andrew Planché (c. 1728–1805) were the first to manufacture soft paste porcelain. They worked in Derby in 1750. A later manufacturer added steatite (soapstone) to the mixture. Then, in 1747, Thomas Frye (1710–1762) of London added bone ash. The

▶ **Complex pottery shapes, such as this coffee pot, are made using slip casting. Slip (a thin, runny mixture of clay and water) is poured into a plaster mold. The water in the slip soaks into the plaster, and the clay left behind becomes more solid. The mold is then broken off, and the clay object is fired.**

▲ *Fine porcelain china is perfect for making expensive tableware. It is light and hard and also glazes well to produce fine decorations.*

use of bone ash as an ingredient became very popular with the famous pottery makers, such as Thomas Minton (1765–1836) and Josiah Spode (1754–1827). In fact, the finest English chinaware is still known as bone china.

One of the famous French porcelains is Sèvres. It became popular throughout the world after 1800, when French chemist and geologist Alexandre Brongniart (1770–1847) took over the factory.

The production of porcelain started in the United States at the end of the eighteenth century. The largest deposits of kaolin are found in Georgia, North Carolina, and Pennsylvania.

Kilns

As well as making pots, kilns are used to harden other mineral objects, such as bricks and enamels. Kilns need to heat these objects to very high temperatures. Therefore they must be made of materials that will not break up from the extreme heat. Firebrick is one such material.

Many kinds of fuel can be used to provide heat for kilns. Wood, coal, oil, and gas are all natural fuels that do the job well. The first fuel used for kilns was wood. Most large industrial kilns are fired by gas jets. Modern potters who work in their own small studios also sometimes prefer wood firing, but many now use electricity. Electric kilns are clean and easy to install and maintain.

Shapes and types

Kilns are built in different shapes. Some are round, some are cone-shaped, and some are rectangular. The two traditional types of kilns—bottle and bank kilns—are both very old in design. Modern kilns have made some changes in their construction, but the same basic rules are still followed.

A bottle kiln has a chamber in which there is a raised platform. This platform is not solid but has air holes or slots in it. Pots are packed on the platform to the height of the chamber wall. They are put into the kiln through an opening, which is sealed with firebrick and clay before firing begins.

In a bank kiln, a cave was dug in a hill and a small doorway was left at the furnace mouth. An opening at the other end of the kiln served as a chimney. The

▲ *Autoglazing is used in china factories that produce large amounts of pottery. The spray of glaze is controlled by a computer. This ensures that just the right amount of glaze is used to produce a smooth and shiny surface on the pottery.*

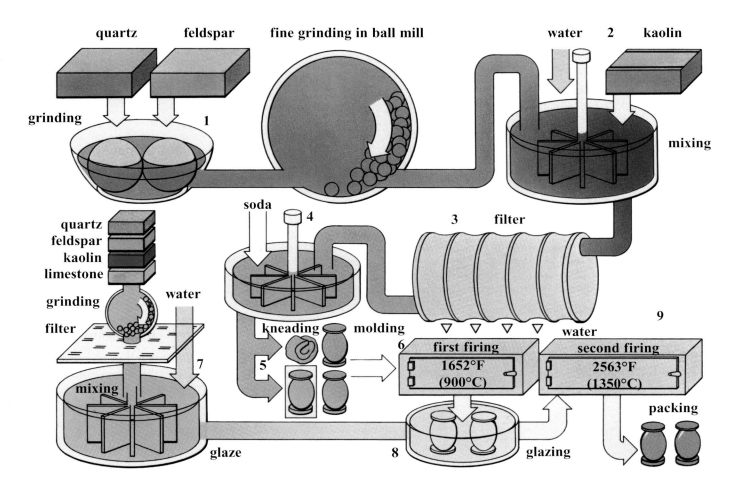

quartz   feldspar   fine grinding in ball mill   water 2 kaolin

grinding   1   mixing

quartz
feldspar
kaolin
limestone

grinding   water   soda 4   3   filter

filter

7   kneading   molding   water   9

5   6 first firing   second firing

mixing   1652°F   2563°F
(900°C)   (1350°C)

packing

glaze   8   glazing

▲ *This diagram shows the stages in making hard paste porcelain. Feldspar and quartz are ground (1) and mixed with kaolin and water (2). This is filtered (3) and mixed with soda (4). After shaping (5), the ware is fired (6). A glaze is made (7) and put on the ware (8). Then it is fired again at a higher temperature (9).*

floor was cut into steps, since the slant of the hill allowed this, and the pots were stacked on the steps. The flames passed around and over the pots. Later, the long, single chamber was broken up into small, separate compartments. This design turned into the modern continuous kiln.

Continuous kilns

Many modern kilns are designed to fire a continuous supply of pottery products. Bricks are fired in a continuous kiln that is similar to the traditional bank kiln. The continuous kiln has a series of separate chambers, and the heat travels from one chamber to the next.

Most pottery is fired in a continuous kiln called the tunnel kiln. Pottery being fired passes slowly through the tunnel on shelves moved by hydraulic power. There are several sections in the tunnel, which is also similar to the tunnel of a bank kiln. In one section, the pottery is heated only gently. In another, the pottery is fired at the correct temperature for its type. In the final section, near the exit, the pottery is cooled.

Kilns used for making pottery do not have to be kept going constantly. They are loaded, fired to reach the necessary temperature, and kept at that temperature for as long as required. The whole kiln is then allowed to cool. When it is cool, the contents are removed, and they are then ready for the next step. In the case of pottery, this would involve glazing and perhaps decorating.

See also: MINERAL • MINING AND QUARRYING

Power

For thousands of years, people have been using the energy of their own muscles and of animals, water, and the wind. Power is the rate at which energy is used up or work is done. People can now measure how much power is needed to do a particular task and construct a machine that will do it quickly and efficiently.

A coiled spring, the batteries in a flashlight, and the gasoline in an automobile engine all possess stored-up energy. If a person releases the spring, switches on the electricity supply to the flashlight, or turns the ignition to create a spark to ignite the gasoline, these systems will release the stored-up energy to do useful work. The rate at which each system does work is called power. The rate of doing work is the same as the rate of conversion of energy, for example, from chemical energy in the gasoline to the kinetic energy of the automobile. However, each system needs only so much energy to complete a job. An airplane, for example, needs more power to lift it off the ground, where it is held by the force of gravity, than is needed to move an automobile along the street.

▼ A competitor strains his muscles to pull a truck during the 1999 World's Strongest Man Competition, held in Prague in the Czech Republic. The greatest muscular power is generated when the largest amount of force is produced in the shortest amount of time.

▶ *The Système International (SI) unit of work is named in honor of English physicist James Prescott Joule, who made many important contributions to the understanding of heat and electricity.*

Measuring force, work, and power

How much work a person does when carrying a bag of groceries up a staircase depends on how high the stairs are and how heavy the load is. Walking up the stairs uses less power running up. The same amount of work done in a shorter time uses more power. This is because the person's weight, as well as the weight of the groceries, is being pulled down by the force of gravity.

Load is the same as force and is measured in units called newtons (N), named in honor of English physicist and mathematician Isaac Newton (1642–1727). Each unit of newton is about the same as the weight of an apple. For each approximate 3 feet (1 meter) an apple is lifted, the person therefore does one newton-meter of work. Work is the same as energy, and the unit of energy is the joule, which is named in honor of English physicist James Prescott Joule (1818–1889). One joule is equal to one newton-meter.

To find out how much work the person carrying the groceries did when climbing the stairs, take his or her mass (weight) and the mass of the groceries, turn it into newtons, and multiply it by the height of stairs climbed (in meters). If the time it took is known, then the power can be calculated. Power output is the number of joules of work done, divided by the time it took to do it (in seconds).

Electrical power

Electrical power is usually measured in units called watts, which is named for Scottish engineer and inventor James Watt (1736–1819). One watt is equal to the rate of working one joule in one second. Usually, electrical power needs a much bigger unit for the more powerful machinery used in industry. The unit chosen is the kilowatt (kW), which is the same as 1,000 watts. Larger units, such as a megawatt (MW), which is 1,000 kilowatts, are used to describe the electrical output of large-scale power plants.

DID YOU KNOW?

Hydroelectric power (HEP) is the power generated from the energy of flowing water. In most HEP plants, a dam is built across a river to trap the water behind in a reservoir. Water can then be released from the reservoir and channeled through a turbine. As the water flows through the turbine, the turbine spins and works a generator to produce electrical power. HEP does not always need a large dam to generate electricity. Some HEP plants use a small chute to channel the river water through a turbine. In other HEP plants, called pumped storage plants, electrical power is used to work the turbines in the opposite direction. They pump water upstream into the reservoir, where it is stored until demand for electrical power is high.

▲ *Electricity illuminates the exterior of Harrods department store in London, England. Electrical power can be thought of as the force required to "push" electrons along a conducting material.*

DID YOU KNOW?

A huge amount of power is required to lift a space shuttle off the launch pad and into space. The mechanical force needed to overcome the weight of the space shuttle and all of its components is called thrust. Thrust is generated by the shuttle's propulsion system. Two solid rocket boosters (SRBs), with a total thrust of about 26 million newtons, provide most of the power to lift the spacecraft off the ground. These are helped by the shuttle's three main engines, which provide the remaining 5.3 million newtons of thrust. The total power output of a space shuttle at takeoff is around 11 billion watts (11 gigawatts), which is equivalent to 15 million horsepower.

Horsepower

Horsepower is the unit of mechanical energy used to describe the power of engines. The term was first used by James Watt, who measured power in terms of the work done by his dray horses. It describes the amount of work done when measured by the distance through which a weight is lifted. One horsepower is the same as 750 watts.

Although the term seems dated, machines and electric motors are still designed to produce a certain amount of horsepower.

See also: ELECTRICITY • ENERGY • FORCES • MASS AND WEIGHT • POWER GENERATION AND DISTRIBUTION • WAVE POWER

Power generation and distribution

The world's first electric power station was designed by U.S. inventor Thomas Edison (1847–1931) and opened in Pearl Street, New York City, in 1882. It brought electricity to about 400 lamps. Since then, power stations have been built all over the world to produce and supply electricity on a huge scale.

Power stations are generally very large buildings in which electric generators produce electrical current. To produce the large amounts of electrical current required, the generators must be driven at high speeds, either by hydroelectric or thermal power. The generators harness this power using turbines. These are circular, rotary (turning) devices with a series of blades or paddles radiating from their centers. Turbines convert the energy of moving fluids into rotary motion. In hydroelectric stations, water turns a turbine. In thermal stations, coal, oil, gas, or nuclear energy is used to heat water to make huge amounts of steam. The steam is kept at high pressure and is released onto the blades of turbines. The spinning turbines turn a central driveshaft, which is connected to an alternator.

Making electricity

It is the alternator that changes the mechanical power of the turbine into electrical power. The main driveshaft of the alternator has magnets fixed to it, and these are spun around inside coils of wire. The movement of the magnets inside the coils causes an electrical current to flow in the wires of the coils. The faster the shaft spins, the higher the voltage produced. From the alternator, the current flows through switches, which can shut off the flow if necessary. The current then passes to a transformer, which greatly increases the voltage. This increase in voltage is necessary because power cables have some resistance to current running through them.

▶ *The concrete domes in this photograph contain the reactors at San Onofre Nuclear Generating Station (SONGS) near Los Angeles, California. SONGS is one of the oldest and simplest nuclear power plants in California, but the plant still provides a significant amount of southern California's electricity.*

This resistance turns some of the current into heat. Low voltages mean more heat, whereas high voltages mean lower heat and only a very small loss of current. Once the voltage has been increased by the transformer, the electricity goes through a network of power cables to wherever it is needed.

THERMAL POWER STATIONS

The majority of thermal power stations are fossil-fuel power stations. They are designed to change the energy stored in the coal, oil, or gas that they burn into electrical energy. Unfortunately, not much more than one-third of the energy of a fuel such as coal can be changed into mechanical energy, even with the most efficient steam boilers and turbines. However, nearly all the mechanical energy can be changed into electrical energy.

The biggest loss of fuel energy comes after the pressurized, high-temperature steam has been used to drive the turbines. The used steam is passed to a condenser, where a constant supply of cold water cools the steam. The biggest heat loss occurs at this stage and can be as high as 40 percent. Very large amounts of cold water are needed to cool the steam. If there is no nearby river large enough to supply the cold water, then the hot water from the condensers is cooled in large concrete water towers.

The fuel used to heat water and create the steam is burned with great efficiency. Oil and natural gas are easily burned, but coal must be ground to a fine powder before burning. The smoke is passed through a dust extractor, which removes the fine, powdery ash. After the ash has been electrified by being passed through a high-voltage wire grid, which makes it easily collected by electrical attraction, it is removed. The ash is put to such uses as making lightweight building materials.

Large coal-burning power stations use enormous amounts of fuel each year. A station producing 2,000 megawatts (2,000 million watts) would need to burn about 4 million tons (3.6 million tonnes) of coal a year, or 2.5 million tons (2.3 million tonnes) of oil.

Gas turbines

Gas turbine generators are often used as simpler, secondary power stations. A gas turbine has three main parts: a compressor, a combustion chamber, and a turbine. The compressor has a fan made of several rows of blades that spin and draw in air. The compressed air becomes hot and is passed into a combustion chamber. Fuel, such as kerosene or natural gas, is spurted into the chamber and burned, producing gases. The burning gases rapidly expand, gushing out of the chamber and spinning the blades of the turbine. An alternator connected to the turbine produces electricity. Gas turbines are limited because much of their heat is lost in the exhaust gases. When a gas turbine is used in a combined cycle power station, however, some of the wasted heat can be put to use.

Combined cycle

Combined cycle power stations make use of the exhaust gases from a gas turbine. The hot exhaust gases are passed to another combustion chamber, this time in a waste-heat boiler. Fuel is mixed and burned with the hot exhaust gases. This heat is used to turn water into steam, which powers a steam-turbine generator (usually called a turbogenerator).

Nuclear power stations

Nuclear power stations use the heat of a nuclear reactor to make the steam needed to work the turbines. Unlike other fuels, however, only a very little nuclear fuel is needed to produce a great amount of heat. Heat from a nuclear reactor is produced from nuclear reactions, when heavy atoms of uranium are blasted with neutrons and split, causing energy to be released. Among the particles set free when the uranium splits are two further neutrons, which collide with more uranium atoms, so releasing more energy. This type of nuclear reaction is called nuclear fission.

There are two kinds of thermal nuclear reactors used in power stations. Water-cooled reactors are more common in the United States, and gas-cooled reactors are more often built in Britain and France. Both water-cooled and gas-cooled nuclear power stations are expensive to build, but because they use so little fuel, the cost of running them is less than half that of coal, oil, and natural gas stations. Nuclear stations are usually kept running all the time, supplying basic (base load) electricity demand.

Water-cooled reactors

Among the water-cooled reactors are the boiling water reactor (BWR) and the pressurized water reactor (PWR). There are also other types, such as the steam-generating heavy water reactor (SGHWR). In a boiling water reactor, uranium, in the form of metal rods, is placed in a vessel of water. A nuclear reaction takes place in the uranium, and the energy given off heats the water and turns it into steam. In a pressurized water reactor, the water in the reactor is kept at high pressure to increase its boiling temperature. It does not turn into steam inside the reactor. Instead, this very hot water is pumped away to a boiler or heat exchanger, where it heats more water and turns that into steam.

Gas-cooled reactors

Some nuclear power plants use carbon dioxide gas (CO_2) as a coolant to remove the heat from the reactor. Electric fans circulate the carbon dioxide around the fuel in the reactor core through a closed-circuit network of pipes. The heated gas pipes then pass into a boiler, where they heat water. The steam from the boiler drives the turbines. Some of the gas-cooled nuclear reactors in use include advanced gas-cooled reactors (AGRs), high temperature reactors (HTRs), and Magnox reactors.

Radiation

In nuclear power stations, the reactor cores and boilers have to be enclosed in thick layers of pre-stressed (especially strengthened) concrete, which protects the power station operators from the

▶ *These wind turbines at the wind farm in San Gorgonio, California, provide clean and renewable energy. However, many turbines are needed to produce significant amounts of electricity.*

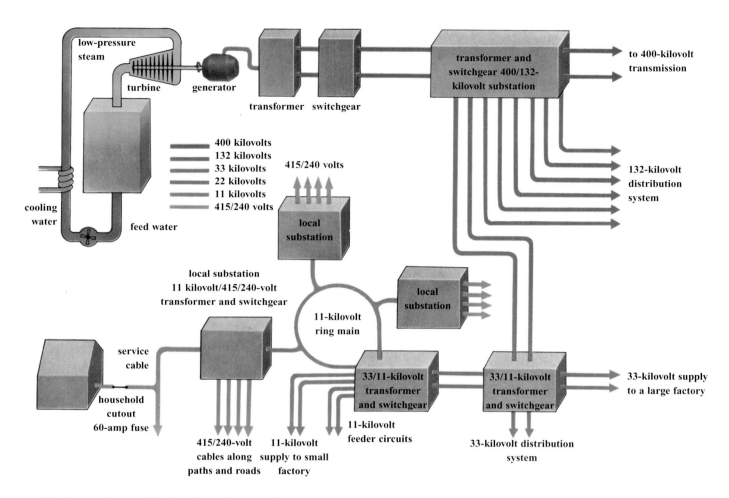

400 kilovolts
132 kilovolts
33 kilovolts
22 kilovolts
11 kilovolts
415/240 volts

▲ *This illustration shows how electricity is distributed from a power station. A transformer steps up the voltage from 22 kilovolts (kv) to 400 kilovolts for the main supply. At substations near areas where the power is to be used, other transformers step the voltage down. Colors indicate the strength of the voltage.*

radiation given off during the nuclear reaction. When the used uranium rods, called irradiated fuel, are removed, they are so dangerous that they have to be taken away in thick lead containers.

RENEWABLE POWER

In many parts of the world, water power is an important means of generating electricity, especially in areas where there are rivers and mountain lakes but little coal, gas, or oil. Water power also has the advantage of being clean and renewable, unlike fossil fuels or nuclear power.

Electricity generated by water is called hydro-electric power (HEP). HEP stations harness the potential energy of stored water. When stored water is released down steep tubes, called penstocks, the powerful rush of water turns the blades of turbines to make electricity. The amount of electricity that can be generated depends on the weight of water available and the head (the distance through which

it falls). The higher the head and the larger the amount of water that can be used, the greater the amount of electricity that can be produced.

Hydroelectric stations are built on rivers, especially those with a steep slope. A dam has to be built to create a large lake behind it, thus giving height to the water. Some of the best places for hydroelectric stations are where rivers flow through gorges or canyons.

Pumped storage

Pumped storage stations are a type of HEP plant, often built between two mountain lakes that lie at different levels. Pumped storage stations use reversible turbines, which not only generate electricity, but also are used as electric motors that turn the turbines as pumps. At night, when demand for electricity is low, water is pumped to the higher lake, where it is kept in readiness for a high demand (peak load) period. At peak load time, the water is run down from the upper lake, through the turbine, to the lower lake.

Wind power

Another way of generating electricity is to harness the power of wind using large wind turbines. The great benefit of wind turbines is that their energy is free, renewable, and they are nonpolluting. They also cause far less ecological damage than other energy sources, including HEP, which requires the flooding of large areas. The energy of wind varies, however, and the electricity generated by wind turbines is unreliable. Also, it takes many wind turbines to produce useful amounts of electricity. So-called "wind farms" cover large areas, creating an unsightly blot on the landscape.

POWER SUPPLY

Demand for electricity changes. At night and on weekends there is usually less electricity used, and the supply during these times of least demand is known as base load. At other times, for example, during a hot summer when air conditioners and fans are in use, demand is at its greatest, and this is known as peak load.

Since electricity cannot be stored on a large scale, power stations must be able to meet the changes in demand. Generally, large power stations that can run on cheap fuel are used to supply the base load. As demand for electricity rises, smaller stations—cheaper to build and easier to start up—are brought into service. These stations, however, are nearly always expensive to run. Gas turbines, for example, are often used in peak load stations. HEP stations, with their huge dams, are very expensive power stations to build but are cheap to run, as the water used is free. HEP stations can be used for either base or peak loads, according to whether or not water is readily available.

AC and DC

In Europe and large parts of the United States, the form of electricity used is known as alternating current (AC). The direction of the alternating current reverses many times a second—so fast, in fact, that it is impossible to detect even a flicker in an electric lightbulb.

Electricity must be sent across distances at very high voltage. The main advantage of AC current is that by using a transformer, the voltage can be reduced at the receiving end to lower, safer amounts. A further important advantage is that it can be sent over long distances in a cable with very little of it wasted.

▲ **This photograph shows the control room of the Kola nuclear power plant in Poljarnye Zori, Russia.**

The other form of electricity is known as direct current (DC), which flows in one direction only. It is more difficult to change the voltage of DC current and make it suitable for small-scale users at the receiving end, so DC current is not as widely used as AC current.

Distributing electricity

A large amount of electricity can be sent through a power cable. There are two main ways of doing this: either a large electrical current (amperage) is pushed by low electrical pressure (voltage), or a

◄ *These electricity pylons carry electricity from a power station through long cables to where it is required. Electricity usually has to travel long distances from power stations to its final destination. The network of electrical supply cables makes up the national grid.*

distances to the people who want to use it in factories, hospitals, schools, and homes. Large cables take the high-voltage electricity from power station transformers either underground or, more often, on tall latticework steel towers called pylons. In towns and cities, the cables are usually laid underground. Overhead cables are made of strands of aluminum (for lightness) wrapped around a steel core (for strength). Although overhead cables are unsightly, they are both cheaper to erect and to maintain over long distances than underground cables. Long ceramic (toughened glass) insulators are fitted to the overhead cables to stop the electricity from flowing to the ground and being wasted or injuring people.

Substations

The main power lines are connected to shorter lines near areas where the power is to be used. The connection is made at a substation, which contains the switch gear, transformers, and instruments to measure the electricity supplied.

The switch gear in the substation contains circuit breakers to close or open the circuit and to cut off very heavy currents that might occur if there is a short circuit. The transformer lowers the voltage from perhaps 132,000 volts to 66,000 or 33,000 volts. From the larger substations, the lower-voltage electricity is carried to a network of other substations. There, the voltage is again stepped down until it reaches the low voltage necessary for home use. In the United States, this is between 110 and 220 volts. Factories and places that need larger amounts of electricity are connected to one of the higher-voltage substations in the network.

small amperage is pushed by a high voltage. Due to the electrical resistance in power cables, and the heating and power losses associated with large amperages and low voltages, a small amperage at as high a voltage as possible is generally the best method. The voltages used to send the electricity from the power stations are different in different countries, but the way it is distributed is roughly the same for all modern power supply systems.

Transformers

Electrical current from generators first goes to a transformer, which steps up (increases) or steps down (decreases) the voltage. Some transformers are very large, and the powerful electrical currents that pass through them make them very hot. For this reason, transformers are usually contained in oil.

Overhead and underground cables

For many reasons, it would be impossible to have power stations built in or near every town and city. Therefore, electrical power has to be brought long

See also: DAM • ELECTRICITY • GAS TURBINE • GENERATOR • HYDROELECTRIC POWER • NUCLEAR REACTOR • TRANSFORMER • TURBINE

Pregnancy and birth

> **Pregnancy is the period of time from conception (fertilization of an egg) to birth (the emergence of the offspring).**

The main indication of pregnancy is a missed menstrual period. Diagnosis can be made two weeks later, either by a medical examination or by using a home-testing kit. These tests work by identifying the presence of a hormone, called human chorionic gonadotropin (hCG), in the woman's urine. Secreted by the embryo seven days after fertilization, it enters the expectant mother's bloodstream and triggers the production of the hormones estrogen and progesterone to prevent her from shedding the lining of the uterus.

After fertilization, the embryo embeds into the lining of the uterus. Cells from the mother's uterus grow and form the placenta to connect the mother to the baby. The placenta is vital, passing nutrients and oxygen to the baby and removing waste products such as carbon dioxide.

A fluid-filled amniotic sac also forms to protect and cushion the embryo. The fluid within the sac helps maintain an even temperature and enables the fetus to move. It is recycled once every three hours and will measure 2 pints (1 liter) at birth.

The trimesters

Pregnancy is usually divided into three sections, called trimesters. The mortality rate during weeks one to twelve, the first trimester, is higher than at any other time of life, with miscarriage occurring in around 20 percent of pregnancies. Sometimes a miscarriage occurs because the placenta fails to function correctly or because the fetus is not developing properly.

▶ *A mother embraces her newborn baby. Newborns have an acute sense of smell, which enable them to recognize the natural scent, or pheromones, as they cuddle up to their mother's body.*

Because all the vital organs of the fetus are formed during the first trimester, the fetus is most vulnerable to environmental factors at that time. Chemicals in the mother's bloodstream may cause problems. For example, alcohol can cause cardiac defects and facial abnormalities. If the mother is infected with a disease such as rubella, the development of the fetus's brain may be impaired. Abnormalities can also be genetic, which means that a disease or condition has been inherited, even though the parents may be unaffected.

Monitoring pregnancy

Special physicians, called obstetricians, care for the expectant mother and fetus once the pregnancy is confirmed. As well as ensuring that the mother is safe, they monitor the development of the fetus to see whether or not it will grow into a healthy baby. Blood-test screening is offered in the early weeks. By checking the levels of proteins in the blood of the pregnant woman, doctors can predict the probability of abnormalities. If problems are suspected, further conclusive tests will be required.

From about the eighth week of pregnancy, the obstetrician may take a sample of structures called chorionic villi from the fetal side of the uterus. These structures are analyzed in the laboratory to

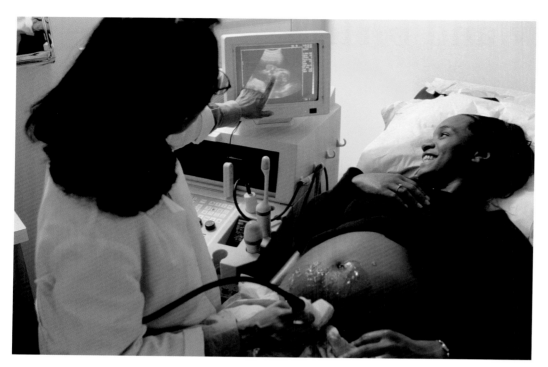

◀ A procedure called ultrasound uses high-frequency sound waves to produce a graphic image of the fetus. This enables the obstetrician to estimate the age of the fetus, identify his or her sex in some cases, and sometimes to identify whether or not there are serious congenital abnormalities, such as Down's Syndrome, and serious diseases, such as spina bifida.

check for abnormalities. A further test, called amniocentesis, is sometimes performed between weeks 14 and 16. It is particularly recommended for women over the age of 35 because of the increased incidence of a condition called Down's syndrome. This process involves the insertion of a needle through the mother's skin into the amniotic sac to remove some living cells shed by the fetus. Some expectant mothers make the difficult decision to terminate a pregnancy if the fetus has a serious disease or condition. Some genetic diseases cannot be detected by tests, however, and both amniocentesis and the chorionic villi tests carry a small risk of miscarriage.

Symptoms of pregnancy

During the early weeks, women often feel unwell due to the production of certain hormones. From week four to week sixteen, morning sickness (nausea) is common and may even cause weight loss. Women may find they have a metallic taste in their mouths, and they are unable to eat food they previously enjoyed. Morning sickness is thought to be caused by increased levels of progesterone and hCG. The release of another hormone, called relaxin, causes lethargy. Its function is to relax the

uterine muscles so that the uterus can expand as the embryo grows. The breasts start to enlarge in preparation for breast-feeding, and the growing uterus may place pressure on the bladder, causing the need to urinate more frequently.

Fetal development

By day 21, the embryo's heart starts to beat and the eyes and ears start to form. By day 28, the brain, gallbladder, intestines, liver, and stomach are developing. In the fifth week, buds that will become the limbs are present. The lungs, lips, and kidneys develop in the sixth week, and the rigid skeleton also starts to form. By week eight, the fetus has most of its features, including fingers and toes. At this stage, the fetus weighs $\frac{1}{28}$ ounce (1 gram) and is 1 inch (2.5 centimeters) long. The heart now beats between 40 and 80 times every minute.

Fingernails, toenails, and genitals have formed by week nine. The kidneys start to produce urine in week ten. Toothbuds start to appear in week 11, by which time the lungs, vocal cords, and liver will have fully formed.

During the second trimester (weeks 13 to 26), the fetus grows rapidly from about 3½ to 9½ inches (8.75 to 23.75 centimeters). The uterus rises out of the pelvis and fills the abdominal cavity. Between week 13 and birth, the mother will gain an average of 20 pounds (9 kilograms). At week 16, she can feel the fetus's arms and legs moving. The fetus is now sensitive to light and sound and has eyelashes and eyebrows. Although the lungs are immature, about 20 percent of babies born at 26 weeks survive with expert medical attention.

In the final trimester, the fetus fills the space inside the uterus, and movement thus becomes limited. The respiratory and circulatory systems attain full development, and the fetus acquires a thin layer of fat below the skin that will offer warmth and protection after birth.

The birthing process

In preparation for birth, the hormone relaxin helps loosen the mother's muscles and tissues so that they are soft and elastic to allow the baby's passage to the outside world. To supply mother and baby with enough oxygen, the breathing rate doubles. Her blood levels increase by 25 percent, providing a reserve if there is excessive bleeding during birth.

Giving birth may take many hours. The process starts with the release of high concentrations of the hormones oxytocin and prostaglandin. These hormones initiate uterine contractions that make the entrance to the uterus, called the cervix, dilate from less than 1 inch (2.5 centimeters) to around 4 inches (10 centimeters). The contractions also push the fetus's head down into the cervix.

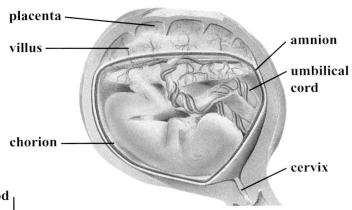

placenta —
villus —
amnion
umbilical cord
chorion —
cervix

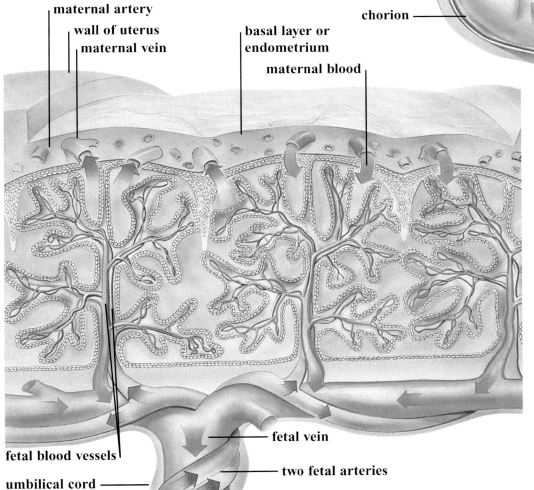

maternal artery
wall of uterus
maternal vein
basal layer or endometrium
maternal blood

fetal vein
fetal blood vessels
two fetal arteries
umbilical cord —

These illustrations reveal the main features of the human placenta. On one side, the placenta is fixed to the wall of the uterus and receives blood vessels from the mother. On the other side, the placenta is attached to the fetus by the umbilical cord. Blood vessels run to and from the fetus through the umbilical cord. The mother's blood transports nutrients and waste products to and from the fetus. Later in the pregnancy, antibodies move from the mother, through the placenta, into the fetus. These antibodies will provide immunity for the baby for about the first six months of his or her life.

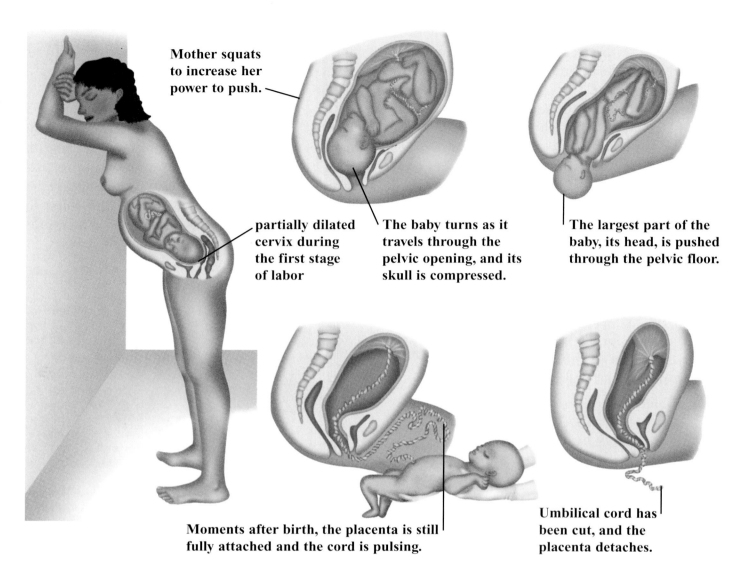

Mother squats to increase her power to push.

partially dilated cervix during the first stage of labor

The baby turns as it travels through the pelvic opening, and its skull is compressed.

The largest part of the baby, its head, is pushed through the pelvic floor.

Moments after birth, the placenta is still fully attached and the cord is pulsing.

Umbilical cord has been cut, and the placenta detaches.

▲ *Keeping upright and active during labor is less painful and more efficient, because gravity works with the uterus to dilate the cervix and push the baby out. During the first stage of labor (1), the cervix dilates and effaces (flattens). In the second stage (2), the baby turns as it is pushed down its mother's vagina. The head then crowns and emerges (3), and the baby is born (4). Finally, the placenta is delivered.*

The uterine contractions start slowly but gradually increase in strength and occurrence. Once they are experienced every ten minutes, women are advised to go to the hospital. It can take up to 20 hours for the active stage of labor to commence. By then, strong and very painful contractions are experienced every two minutes. The baby is only slightly smaller than the pelvic opening, and the mother must push with both her abdominal and her uterine muscles to give birth. As the mother pushes, the soft skull of the baby compresses as it passes through the birth canal.

The head usually appears first, and the body follows soon after. The umbilical cord is then cut. Most doctors advise that the mother breast-feeds immediately, because this prompts the expulsion of the placenta through the vagina. In the days that follow, the muscles of the uterus continue to contract until the uterus returns to its original size.

See also: ENDOCRINE SYSTEM • GENETICS • MEDICAL IMAGING • MEDICAL TECHNOLOGY • REPRODUCTIVE SYSTEM • ULTRASONICS

Pressure

Pressure is the ratio of the force applied to a surface to the area of the surface. The atmosphere exerts pressure on everything on the surface of the planet. Objects on Earth also exert pressure on their surroundings. Solids apply pressure in one direction only, but liquids and gases exert pressure in all directions.

If two people of exactly the same weight walk on deep snow, one wearing boots and the other snowshoes, the person in boots will sink deeper than the person in snowshoes. The weight of the person in boots is concentrated underneath the soles of the boots. Someone in snowshoes has spread the same weight over an area several times larger, so this person does not sink into the snow.

Following the same principle, thumb tacks have a large flat area for a thumb to push on and a point on the other side. The flat side spreads the force of a person's thumb over a larger area, and the sharp point concentrates this force into a tiny spot to make it sink in.

Pressure is a measure of force or weight per unit area. In the Imperial system, pressure is measured in pounds (lb.) per square inch (psi). In the metric system, pressure is measured in pascals (Pa). One pascal is equal to one newton per square meter (N/m^2). One newton is the force required to accelerate one kilogram one meter per second.

Pressure in fluids

Fluids (liquids and gases) behave differently from solids. If the weight of a fluid is ignored, then a fluid under compression will have the same pressure throughout, because the molecules of a fluid are free to move around. If there were parts of a fluid at a higher pressure, the molecules would quickly shuffle around until the pressure was the same throughout the fluid.

▶ *These balloons are filled with pressurized gas. The balloons have inflated because the pressure of the gas inside them is high enough to balance the resistance of the rubber and the atmospheric pressure acting outside.*

However, pressure in fluids is not quite so straightforward, because fluids have weight. This means that in a column of fluid, the fluid toward the bottom is under more pressure than the fluid at the top. The weight of the fluid increases pressure with depth. The effect is like trying to take a book from the bottom of a stack of books—it is much harder than taking a book from the top of the stack.

Unlike a stack of books, however, the fluid in a column exerts pressure on the sides of the column as well as downward. At any one depth, the pressure is the same in all directions. This pressure exerted equally in all directions within a confined fluid is called hydrostatic pressure.

Atmospheric pressure

Gas in a column also exerts a pressure. However, gases have much less density (less weight for the same volume) than liquids, so there is no depth effect unless the column is very large. Only a quantity of gas as large as that which makes up Earth's atmosphere (which is held around the planet by gravity) has a measurably greater pressure at the bottom than higher up. At sea level, atmospheric pressure is given as 14.7 psi (101,350 Pa). At the top of Mount Everest (an altitude of 29,028 feet or 8,848 meters), atmospheric pressure has been measured at about 4.65 psi (32,073 Pa). Although atmospheric pressures are high, people and other life on Earth do not even notice them.

Pressure gauges

Pressure gauges are instruments that measure the pressure of liquids or gases. The first pressure gauge was made by Italian scientist Evangelista Torricelli (1608–1647) in 1643, and it was used to measure the pressure of the atmosphere. Other gauges have since been produced that have made modern instruments increasingly accurate.

▼ *These illustrations show how pressure is exerted in a solid, a liquid, and a gas. A weight spread over a large area (top) will exert less pressure than the same weight confined to a smaller area. In a liquid (bottom left), the pressure at the bottom of the column is greater than at the top, because the liquid at the bottom has more liquid above it pressing it down. However, the pressure at any one point must be the same in all directions. Otherwise, the molecules of the liquid would rearrange themselves until they had equalized the pressure. More molecules of gas in a container (bottom right) produce more pressure, because there are more molecules to bounce off each other and off the sides of the container.*

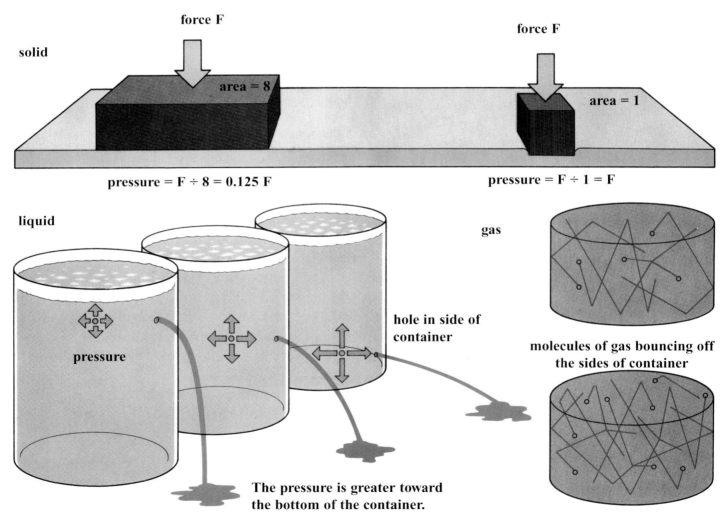

force F

solid

area = 8

force F

area = 1

pressure = F ÷ 8 = 0.125 F

pressure = F ÷ 1 = F

liquid

pressure

gas

hole in side of container

molecules of gas bouncing off the sides of container

The pressure is greater toward the bottom of the container.

With more molecules per unit volume, there are more collisions and the pressure is greater.

To determine the pressure of a liquid or gas, its force is divided by the area over which it exerts its force. The answer is called the absolute pressure. Since most pressure gauges work in atmospheric pressure, they show the actual (absolute) pressure minus atmospheric pressure. This is known as gauge pressure. The difference between two measured pressures is known as differential pressure.

Bourdon tube gauges

One of the most common and useful pressure gauges is the Bourdon tube gauge. It was named for its inventor, French engineer Eugène Bourdon (1808–1884). It has an oval tube of thin, slightly elastic metal bent into an arc like a letter C. One end is sealed; the other end can be attached to the container filled with pressurized liquid or gas. As the pressure flows, the tube starts to straighten out. As the sealed end starts to move upward, it pulls on a pointer. The pointer moves over a scale marked in degrees of pressure. Bourdon tubes are also sometimes shaped as spirals and twists.

Diaphragms, capsules, and bellows

A diaphragm pressure gauge has a container, one surface of which is a thin, springy metal disk. The pressure of the gas or liquid to be measured forces the thin metal to bulge slightly and to move a pointer. Sometimes two corrugated (furrowed) diaphragms are welded together into a circular envelope called a capsule. The gas or liquid is fed into the capsule, and the movement registers on a dial.

A number of capsules, one on top of the other like a bellows, are used in some gauges, such as aneroid barometers. The bellows expands or contracts with the pressure, and an attached lever moves a pointer or pen.

Electronic pressure gauges

Pressure gauges that use mechanical linkages are most useful for measuring static pressures or pressures that change slowly. For pressures that change rapidly, electrical pressure transducers are more suitable. These are devices that can sense changing pressures and produce a proportional

▲ *The nitrogen in this storage tank is stored at very high pressure to keep it in its liquid state. The gauges on the top of the tank monitor and regulate the pressure inside the tank to prevent it from exploding.*

electric output signal. Such electrical pressure gauges include strain gauges and inductance, reluctance, capacitance, and piezoelectric devices. Electromechanical transducers convert changes in pressure of fluids to electrical signals. These are used to control hydraulic systems.

See also: ATMOSPHERE • BAROMETER • FORCES •
HYDRAULICS • MASS AND WEIGHT •
PIEZOELECTRICITY • TRANSDUCER

Printed circuit

A printed circuit is a pattern made of copper on a board. The printed circuit is used to connect the parts that work an electronic device. Copper can do this because it is a good conductor—electricity can move through copper from one substance and into another.

Before the 1950s, the components of an electronic device were mounted on a frame. The connections were made from each component by soldering lengths of insulated wire between them. In a large device, there might be hundreds of pieces of wire to be soldered in this way. It took many hours of work, and mistakes were easily made. As a result, electronic devices were expensive to manufacture and therefore to buy.

The printed circuit was the answer. A board made of an insulating material was covered with a layer of copper. A pattern was then printed on the copper in a substance that would not be attacked by acid. This pattern was the circuit itself. The parts of the copper that were not needed in the circuit were then etched away with acid. This left the circuit as a pattern of copper securely fixed to the insulating board. The various parts were then soldered to the copper to form the electronic device.

In practice, holes were drilled in the board so that the components could be mounted on the side of the board without the conductive copper traces and the wires taken through to be soldered to the conducting copper on the other side.

Modern printed circuit boards often have copper on both sides. Some are even built up in several layers of copper-conductor patterns with layers of insulating material between them. The boards themselves are made of tough plastic or fiberglass.

Integrated circuits

The integrated circuit (IC) was a development of the printed circuit board and of the technology of the transistor. Transistors are made by diffusing (passing) one material into another. Hundreds of transistors can be made at once on a single wafer of silicon. Other components, such as capacitors and diodes, can be made in similar ways.

◀ This photograph shows the conductive traces and electronic components on a printed circuit board. A technique called surface mounting is used to solder the components directly onto the surface of the board.

◄ *A technician inspects a circuit board using a video light microscope fitted with a charge-coupled device (CCD) camera. The close-up image obtained by the camera is displayed on a television monitor.*

Many different components can be mixed together on a silicon wafer to make a circuit. The circuit is built up on a base of one semiconductor material, called a substrate. A layer of another type of material is then "grown" on the base. This second layer is covered with a layer of oxide, and gaps are cut into the oxide. More material may be passed through the gaps to set individual areas of the material apart in the second layer.

This process of building up material, etching away parts of the surface, and passing material into the layers below may continue. All the different components of a complete working circuit can then be connected by an aluminum layer.

Dozens of components can be combined in a single IC the size of a pinhead. As a result, many electronic circuits can be placed in a tiny space. The power used by ICs is often tiny, too, although the output is also very small. Another advantage of the very tiny size of these devices is that they work very quickly. The electrons do not have as far to go between the components. This property is very useful in devices such as microprocessors that work at speeds of millions of operations per second.

Thick and thin film circuits

Since the power output of an IC is small, the capacitor and resistor values that come from IC techniques are also limited. Where larger values are needed, thick or thin film circuits are used.

Thick film circuits are made by printing the circuit onto a base with an ink that conducts electricity. Ink is forced onto the base through a photographic stencil supported on a screen of fine wire mesh. After printing, the ink is bonded firmly onto the base by firing it in a furnace.

Thin film circuits are made by dropping pure metal onto a ceramic or glass base in a vacuum. First, the metal is put in a chamber with the base. A vacuum is created and the chamber is then heated until the metal "boils off." The metal forms a solid again on the cold surface of the base material. The base is covered with metal masks so that the metal can solidify on the base only through the openings in the masks, which follow the lines of the circuit.

See also: ELECTRONICS • ELECTRON TUBE • MICROELECTRONICS • TRANSISTOR

Printing

People are surrounded by things that have been printed, such as drawings, photographs, stamps, money, and decorations—and, most importantly, printed words. These are in books, magazines, newspapers, directories, maps, and signs—all the items people depend on for information of every kind each day of our lives.

▲ *The first writing was probably cuneiform, which was developed in Sumeria (present-day Iraq) about five thousand years ago. Cuneiform was written with a triangular stick, which was used to make marks in a tablet or disk of soft clay. The clay hardened so the writing could be easily transported and stored. Without printing technology, however, the Sumerians had to write out each passage of text by hand.*

Of course, people take printing for granted now because printing presses have been around for more than five hundred years. However, before the press was invented, only a few people owned books or even learned how to read and write.

In the modern world, many things are printed, including paper money, cash-register receipts, newspapers, and official forms and certificates. Many paintings and other pictures are reproduced by lithography (a form of printing) so that people can have copies to hang on the wall.

The word *print* comes from earlier English and French words meaning "to press." The design of the first presses used in Europe was based on an oil press, used to squeeze oil from olives.

Originally, a printed copy of something was made by spreading ink onto its surface and pressing paper against it. At first, images and symbols were printed. Then, letters, or type, were used to print words. Now modern printers do not make an impression of type; they produce images and text that have been put together by computer software.

Early printing

The first type of printing was achieved by pressing colorful patterns onto cloth. It is believed that this was first done in India more than two thousand years ago. The Indians printed onto fine, white cotton with patterns cut into a wooden block. The pattern was in relief, that is, sticking up above the surface of the rest of the block. The patterns were covered with dye, and the block was pressed down onto stretched cloth. Most of the early patterns were simple designs that could be pressed down over and over again to make a continuous pattern on a single piece of cloth.

The Chinese began printing on paper about 2,500 years ago. They were already writing on paper in black ink using fine brushes. The Chinese ink was a mixture of soot and gum. It was made into a solid block, and water was added to make the ink liquid as it was needed.

By 400 CE, the Chinese were printing their names on documents using stone or metal stamps. Their signatures were carved into the surfaces of the stamps. These were then coated in red dye and pressed onto the document. Black ink could not be used because it did not stick to the stamps very well. Black ink does stick to wood, however, so woodblocks were used to make black prints.

The words and pictures of books were carved into blocks of wood and printed on paper. The world's earliest book was printed in this way. The *Diamond Sutra* was filled with Buddhist teachings. It was produced in 868 CE in China. This book was not bound into many pages, as with modern books. Instead, it was a long scroll measuring 1 foot (30 centimeters) wide and 16 feet (5 meters) long.

Movable type

By the eleventh century, Chinese writing was being printed with movable type. These were made of wood, and small woodblocks represented each Chinese letter. The blocks were arranged to make new passages of text, which was easier than carving a new page from scratch. The blocks could also be used many times for printing different texts.

Movable type has been traced to two Chinese inventors. One was Pi Sheng, who molded type in clay in 1042. The other was Wang Chen, who used wood for the type in 1314. However, the invention of movable type did not cause a huge explosion of printing in China as it did in Europe. This may be partly because there are 40,000 characters used in Chinese writing, a great many for printers to learn and handle. On the other hand, the Roman alphabet, which is used for most European languages, has only 26 letters. Having only 26 pieces of type makes printing a much simpler job.

The Gutenberg mystery

The first European to use movable type was German inventor Johannes Gutenberg (1400–1468). Little is known about Gutenberg, and no works are signed by him. It is thought that he started to experiment with printing around 1436. At some time during the next 12 years or so, he set up a print shop in Mainz, Germany. The money was put up by his business partner, German goldsmith Johann Fust (1400–1466).

▶ *This picture is a print made from a block of wood. Japanese artist Munakata Shiko cut the image into the wood and then painted on colored inks before making the print. Simpler woodblocks were used in China and Korea to print words for nearly one thousand years.*

In 1456, Gutenberg produced the famous 42-line Bible. This book was so called because almost every page has two columns of 42 lines each. The printing was as good as the best handwritten manuscript of the day, and this Bible is still one of the finest books ever printed. Gutenberg printed two hundred copies. Most were printed on paper, but a few were printed on vellum, which is made from lambskin.

Gutenberg's press was similar to a screw press used in Europe since Roman times, which was used to squeeze oil from olives or juice from grapes. A page of type was arranged in a wooden frame and then coated in ink. A piece of paper was then placed on the type and both were placed in the press. A heavy block was then screwed down onto the form so it pressed onto the paper. Despite the quality of his work, Gutenberg's business did not succeed. After a few years, Fust's son-in-law, Peter Schöffer (1425–1502), took over the print shop.

Within 30 years of Gutenberg's death, printing had spread throughout Europe. For many years, most printers went to Germany to learn the trade. The first English printer was William Caxton (1422–1491), who trained in Cologne, Germany. Caxton opened a shop in London in 1476 near Fleet Street, which eventually became famous as the street of newspapers.

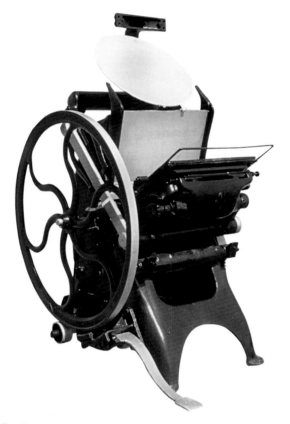

▲ *Early printing presses relied on each piece of paper being printed by hand. The type was coated in ink, and then the paper was pressed onto it. In this way, an impression of the type was produced by the ink.*

Printing came to the New World in 1539, when Italian printer Juan Pablos (died ca. 1561) produced the first book in Mexico City. In 1640, the first book in the North American colonies that would eventually become the United States was printed in Cambridge, Massachusetts. It was the *Bay Psalm Book*, which was a hymn book used by the Massachusetts Bay Colony.

Printing press developments

The earliest presses were made of wood and had a screw top. The top had to be worked by hand, and this took great strength. To add to the difficulties, the printing area was so small that only half a page could be done each time. So every full page required the press to be worked twice.

One of the improvements made to presses in the sixteenth century was the use of metal instead of wood for the screw. Another important advance was the sliding bed, which meant that the form could be slid under the block. This innovation sped up the printing process.

In 1800, English inventor Charles Stanhope (1753–1816) made the first all-iron printing press. The press used a system of levers that made it easier to use than a screw press. The Stanhope press also had a printing area large enough to handle a page at a time, so it doubled the printing speed. It also improved the quality of the printed page.

German printer Friedrich König (1774–1833) was the first to design a steam-powered press. His press, built in 1806, could make four hundred impressions an hour. This was only the beginning of König's improvements to printing presses. Five years later, he patented the cylinder press. This type of press had a revolving cylinder that met the paper on the sliding bed as it moved backward and forward automatically. The paper was also automatically placed on the bed and removed after printing. This press produced eight hundred sheets an hour. In 1813, another König invention further improved the printing process. This was a press that could print both sides of a sheet at once.

Typesetting

For more than four hundred years after the invention of the printing press, arranging the type to be printed was the job of the compositor. Compositors were craftspeople that took every letter, one at a time, from type cases and arranged them into words and sentences. The capital letters—used at the beginning of sentences—were taken from the upper case, while the smaller letters came from the lower case. People still refer to these two groups of type as upper case and lower case.

Compositors arranged letters (and the spaces between words) in a handheld container called a composing stick. The sticks were then arranged one on top of each other into a page, and this arrangement was called a form. The form was then locked into a frame called a chase.

The shape of the piece of type was a mirror (back to front) image of the printed letter. This produced a print that faced the correct way. Compositors had to work backward and arrange letters from right to left, so they would be printed from left to right on the page. Manual typesetting required great skill and took a long time to complete.

Compositors are no longer needed to set type. Instead, the process is controlled by a computer (see page 1359).

Stereotyping

The next important change in printing technology revolutionized newspaper printing. In the late eighteenth century, stereotype was developed. A stereotype was a single metal plate that could be used to print a whole page of text. (The word *stereotype* can also mean a set of fixed ideas about things or people. This meaning came after the original printing term, since stereotyped plates are always the same.) The plates could be curved to fit around a roller. These were used on a rotary press, which prints from a continuous roll of paper. The roll was then cut into individual pages. Stereotype plates made it possible to produce thousands of identical prints quickly. They were also sturdier than type arranged in forms and did not wear out as quickly. Rotary presses with stereotypes could produce an average of 50,000 copies an hour.

Stereotypes were made by pouring molten metal into a mold of the form. The metal copy that resulted was a strong and flexible single sheet.

The first step was to make the mold. This was done by placing a sheet of heavy paper pulp on top of the printing form. The pulp and the form were

▼ *Newspapers are printed on huge rolls of thin paper called newsprint. Stereotyped plates were used until the end of the 1980s, when phototypesetting became a popular alternative.*

▲ *A compositor arranges lines of type on a plate. The individual letters have already been converted into a line of words, called a slug, by a Linotype machine.*

then placed into a molding press. The pulp and the form were squeezed together until an exact impression of the form was made on the moistened paper pulp. This was called a mat.

The mat was curved into a semicircle, dried, and heated in an oven until it hardened. During the baking stage, the mat shrank because the moisture was removed. It was important that the mat did not shrink too much.

The next step was to cast the metal plate. The curved mat was put into a casting machine, and molten metal was poured onto it. The metal used was mainly lead, but it also contained antimony and tin. The casting machine then cooled the plate and shaved off any extra bits of metal.

Several stereotypes of the same page were made at one time using the same mat. This allowed the same newspaper to be printed on several presses at once. Plates were also sent across the country, so the newspapers could be printed in several places.

Newspapers were printed in black and white using stereotype plates until the late 1980s. Modern newspapers are printed in color by phototypesetting.

Further advances

At the end of the nineteenth century, an invention made typesetting much easier. German-born U.S. inventor Ottmar Mergenthaler (1854–1899) led the way by inventing the first automatic typesetting machine in Baltimore, Ohio, in 1884. He called it a Linotype. The operator of the Linotype uses a keyboard to tap out words in a similar way to a computer keyboard. As each letter is tapped out, a brass mold representing the letter drops into a frame. The molds then line up to form a row of letters and spaces. When all the letters that will fit onto one line have dropped into position, they are filled with molten metal into a solid piece of type called a slug. The slugs are then arranged into a page form as before. Automatic typesetters greatly increased the speed of printing, and newspapers soon began to use them. The *New York Tribune* was the first to use a Linotype in 1886.

In 1887, U.S. inventor Tolbert Lanston (1844–1913) patented another automatic typesetting machine, called the Monotype. It had two units, the first of which was operated by a keyboard. This punched coded perforations onto a spool of paper. The spool fed into the second unit, which cast and assembled the letters mechanically. The process was similar to manual typesetting but much faster.

The Ludlow machine, which was used for large-size type and special print styles, dates from 1905. It combined manual and machine typesetting. The compositor set the letters in a composing stick that was then inserted into the Ludlow's casting unit. One or more slugs of type were cast at once and then arranged in order for printing.

Lithography

Printers call the printing method that involves pushing type against paper letterpress. Letterpress was the method developed by Gutenberg. Since then, other printing methods have been developed, including gravure and lithography.

Lithography uses the fact that grease and water do not mix. In lithography, part of the plate to be printed is greased so that it will take the ink. The part that will not be printed is kept wet so that it will not take the ink. In this way, images can be printed from a flat plate. Before the development of digital printing, lithography was often used to print fine art and is often still used for this purpose.

Lithography was developed by German printer Aloys Senefelder (1771–1834). In 1798, he began printing images drawn onto a highly polished slab of stone. (The word *lithography* comes from the Greek word *lithikos,* which means "stone," and the Latin *graphus,* meaning "picture.") Plates can now be made of metal, plastic, or paper. Some artists prefer to use stone for making prints. Senefelder discovered lithography by accident. He was working in Munich, Germany, and used a form of limestone found in the area. The image to be printed was drawn directly onto the stone with a crayon.

The first lithography presses were flatbeds. They kept the plate and the paper flat. In 1900, rotary presses holding curved aluminum plates were introduced. Litho plates must be thin and strong. Aluminum is still favored, although zinc is sometimes used.

On lithography presses, a fountain is used to dampen the areas of the plate that are not going to be printed. The inking rollers release a film of ink from a reservoir to the areas that will be printed. One of the difficulties in lithography is balancing the amounts of water and ink.

Modern lithography uses aluminum plates produced by photographic methods. The plates can be positive or negative, as in photography. The positive plates are used for runs of about 100,000, and the negative plates for runs of about 50,000.

In offset lithography, the printing is carried out on rotary presses. The plate does not transfer the ink directly onto the paper. Instead, the ink is offset

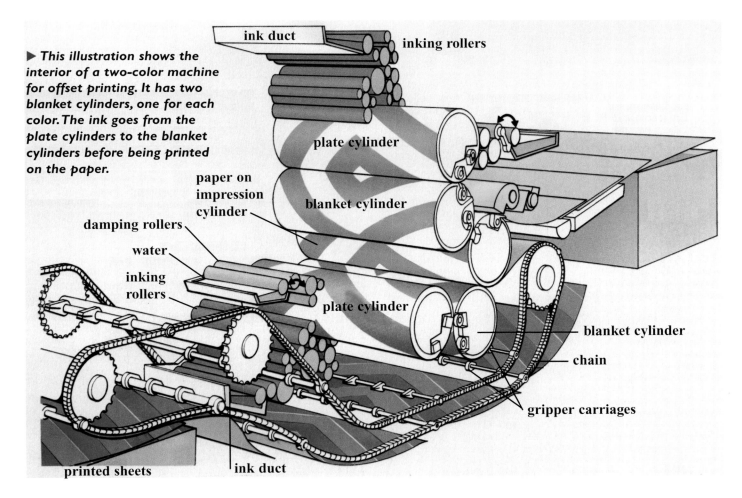

▶ **This illustration shows the interior of a two-color machine for offset printing. It has two blanket cylinders, one for each color. The ink goes from the plate cylinders to the blanket cylinders before being printed on the paper.**

ink duct

inking rollers

plate cylinder

blanket cylinder

paper on impression cylinder

damping rollers

water

inking rollers

plate cylinder

blanket cylinder

chain

gripper carriages

printed sheets

ink duct

▲ *Computers are used to arrange words and images before printing. All text and nearly all images are now prepared for printing using computers.*

from the plates onto a rubber-covered blanket cylinder. This transfers the ink onto the paper (see the illustration on page 1357).

In offset printing, different colored inks are applied to the paper by different blanket cylinders. Each blanket cylinder picks up an impression from a single plate, which contains an image of the area of the page that is covered by one particular color. A color offset printer generally uses four blanket cylinders, one representing each color of ink. However, some color offset printers may use five inks. If they are printing unusual colors, such as gold or silver, or if parts of the page are being coated with plastic, the offset printer will require extra blanket rollers.

The gravure method

In gravure printing, the text and images to be printed are lower than the surface of the plate. Historically, this was used to print very close copies of images using strong colors. However, it was expensive and was only used for title pages of books and other detailed images. Artists may still use gravure printing for high-quality print effects.

Gravure was invented in England in 1895 by Czech printer Karl Klietsch (1841–1927). The plates used for gravure printing are made of copper, and the design is formed from tiny dots recessed in the surface using chemicals. The recessed (lowered) areas are filled with ink. The upper surface of the plate is then wiped clean between every impression that is made.

Phototypesetting

In all the printing methods, plate making is an important part of the process. Different kinds of plates are needed for the different methods, depending on whether printing is from a flat, raised, or sunken surface. However, the principle is the same. In the past, molten metal was used to cast plates. Now a photographic process called photo-typesetting is used to make plates.

Phototypesetting uses films to make plates. First, the original text and images are prepared as films. The films are produced on transparent (see-through) plastic. They may be negative or positive images of the original. Black-and-white pages are recreated as a single film. Color pages are split into four colors—cyan (turquoise), magenta (purple), yellow, and black. These are the four inks used in color printing.

The plates used for printing onto paper are made of flexible metal or plastic and coated with a light-sensitive substance. To make a record of the text and images on the printing plate, light is shone through the positive or negative films and onto the plate. How much light gets through to the light-sensitive substance on the printing plate depends on the light and dark areas of the films. Light areas on the films allow more light through to the printing plate. As the light hits the light-sensitive coating on the plate, a reaction takes place, and the light-sensitive substance hardens. Dark areas on the films do not allow as much light through. As a result, the areas of light-sensitive coating on the plate do not harden and can be washed away. In this way, the hardened coating forms a record of the text and images on the films. Parts of the plate not covered by the coating are then removed by acids to produce a raised area on the plate. The plate is then ready for printing onto paper.

The printing revolution

In the modern world, printing is now controlled by computers. Word processors and other computer software are used to arrange text and images on screen. This process is known as pre-press. Early pre-press systems used codes to arrange the size and position of items on the page. By the early 1990s, all computer programs were WYSIWYG, which stands for "what you see is what you get."

Desktop printers can print directly from a computer, without the need for films and plates. Many use a grid of ink nozzles to squirt colored inks into a pattern. Others work like photocopiers. Desktop printers produce copies of a lower quality than printing presses. They are used for small jobs but not, for example, printing books.

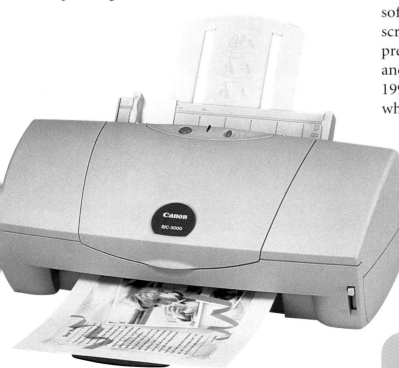

◀ *This printer uses jets of color ink to recreate the image seen on the computer screen.*

See also: COMPUTER • KEYBOARD AND TYPEWRITER • PHOTOCOPIER • PHOTOGRAPHY • PHOTOGRAPHY, DIGITAL

Propeller

Vessels that travel through water or air often use propellers to move them along. A propeller is a spiral-shaped device that provides forward thrust by pushing water or air behind it at speed. To do its job properly, a propeller has to be designed for the size, shape, and speed of the vessel it will be moving.

Propellers were first used in the 1850s to propel ships. Engines had been developed that were suitable for powering ships, and propellers were found to be the most efficient way of changing the energy produced by a ship's engine into the necessary thrust to push the vessel through the water. Since engine-powered ships do not rely on the wind for their power, propeller-driven ships soon began to replace sailing ships.

The flow of water around a ship's propeller, which is at the stern (back) of the ship, is affected by the shape of the ship's hull (body) and its speed. When the ship moves forward, it drags some of the surrounding water with it. This field of flow is called the wake field. The wake field varies across the propeller, so that the turning blade will pass through areas of water moving at variable speeds. This unevenness makes the propeller vibrate, and this vibration must be avoided.

Cavitation

The passage of the water means that there is a lot of pressure behind the propeller and far less pressure in front of it. The low pressure creates pockets that contain only water vapor. These look like bubbles of air, and they form a spiral the same shape as the propeller. The propeller is then no longer moving water, but pockets filled with a tiny amount of water vapor. This is called cavitation. It does not help to move the ship and is a further cause of unwanted propeller vibration.

▲ This propeller on a U.S. warship is being checked in a navy dockyard. Propellers must be carefully maintained to provide the best performance.

Design and construction

A ship's propeller has to move the ship in the most efficient way, and it must be strong enough not to break under the strain. The propeller must be at its most efficient when the ship is at cruising speed, but it must also be able to work well when the ship is getting up to speed or if it must increase speed for some other reason.

The angle of the blades is called the pitch, and the pitch is usually varied over the blade to form a curve. The pressure on the water thus increases gradually as the propeller turns, reducing the chance of cavitation.

▶ *This photograph shows a U.S. Air Force aircraft technician conducting a preflight check on the variable pitch propeller of an aircraft before takeoff.*

Most conventional propellers have two blades, but some have four or even six. The controllable pitch propeller has its blades mounted separately on a hub. The blades can be swiveled mechanically from inside the ship's engine room, thus changing the pitch and allowing the ship's speed to be changed without changing the speed of the engine.

Airplane propellers

Airplane propellers work on the same basic principle as ship propellers. They must be much larger and faster, however, because air is much lighter than water, and more of it has to be moved in order to move the airplane. Also, an airplane does not float in air, as a ship does in water, so it has to be kept from falling.

Airplane blades have an airfoil shape similar to that of the wings. They are designed to give a lift effect, called thrust, to counteract the resistance, called drag. To achieve high thrust and low drag, the shape and angle of the blades must be carefully designed to provide the correct angle of attack.

Small, single-engined airplanes usually have fixed pitch propellers. Their speed is varied by changing the engine speed. Larger airplanes have variable pitch propellers to meet the different demands of speed, altitude, and engine speed. Both kinds of propellers usually work most efficiently at one particular speed.

Pitch and thrust

Large airplanes have over 100 degrees of pitch control. These range from feathering, where the blades are parallel to the airstream, giving the least drag (essential if an engine should fail), to coarse pitch (for high speeds and altitudes), fine pitch (for takeoff), disking (for zero thrust), windmilling, and reverse thrust (used for braking).

The tips of the propeller blades move through the air faster than the base of the blades. If the engine speed is greatly increased, this could cut the air at supersonic speeds (speeds faster than sound),

which is inefficient in conventional airplanes. So, instead of using longer propeller blades, larger airplanes have more blades—up to five instead of the usual two. The blades can also be made wider. However, there is a practical limit to the width and number of blades, and propeller-driven airplanes usually fly at a top speed of around 400 miles (650 kilometers) per hour.

Materials and manufacture

Ship propellers are generally cast from alloys, usually mixtures of aluminum and nickel or bronze and manganese. Airplane propellers, originally made from laminated wood (composed of thin layers), now consist of light, modern materials. These include steel with a honeycomb inner structure, and special kinds of plastics.

See also: AIRPLANE • ALLOY • SHIP AND SHIPBUILDING • TURBINE

Prosthetics

Prosthetics is a branch of medicine that deals with the production and application of artificial body parts. Prosthetics also refers to the artificial body parts themselves, although they are more commonly known as prostheses. Prostheses allow many physically disabled people to live more normal lives.

Prostheses (*singular*, prosthesis) are typically used to replace body parts lost by injury (traumatic), missing from birth (congenital), or to supplement defective body parts. The origin of prosthetics as a branch of medicine is attributed to the sixteenth-century French surgeon Ambroise Paré (1510–1590), who created artificial hands and arms for wounded soldiers. Further improvements in the design of prostheses have largely been in response to the many casualties of warfare. By the middle of the twentieth century, after the two world wars, lightweight materials and sophisticated mechanical joints had been introduced. The greatest advances, however, have been made in the twenty-first century, by bioengineers who have improved the function of prostheses and developed synthetic (human-made) materials that can be integrated into the human body without being rejected. These are called biocompatible materials. Bioengineers have also improved the look of prosthetics, making them increasingly lifelike. They often have silicone rubber coverings, shaped exactly like the biological body part.

The range of modern prostheses available includes artificial hands, limbs, eyes, ears, and teeth, as well as replacement biocompatible materials for the heart, kidneys, skin, and blood. The term *prostheses* may also be used for such devices as eyeglasses, hearing aids, and pacemakers. These do not replace body parts but improve their function.

▲ *Dominique André (1405) of France and Neil Fuller (1408) of Australia race in the men's 200-meter amputee final at the World Athletics Championships in 2001. Fuller won with a time of 23.32 seconds—only a couple of seconds slower than the able-bodied athletes.*

Artificial limbs and joints
Artificial limbs are used to replace limbs that have been removed by surgery, often because of injury, infection, or poor blood supply. They can also be used by some people born without limbs.

When someone loses an arm or a leg, doctors and bioengineers can now give the patient a new artificial limb that looks and works very much like the lost one. Many amputees are able to move around almost normally and enjoy an active life.

New, strong, light alloys (metal mixtures), plastics, ceramics, and composite materials have helped people who design artificial limbs improve both the function and appearance of the limbs. Some of the most useful materials now used for those needing joint replacement are titanium alloys and carbon fiber.

Titanium alloys can be used to form "new" shoulder, elbow, hip, and knee joints. Titanium is strong, lightweight, and nonmagnetic, and it resists corrosion. Most important for implantation (inserting inside the body), titanium is compatible with living tissue and will not irritate or harm any parts of the body with which it comes into contact. Carbon fiber composites are increasingly being used in artificial limbs, largely because of their superior strength-to-weight characteristics.

Artificial limbs can be divided into two groups— unpowered and powered. Unpowered limbs rely on the movements of the patient's body for their control. Powered limbs have more complex hinges and joints with electronic controls.

Artificial legs

For artificial legs, unpowered limbs are usually still used. A person's legs must support the weight of the whole body and allow him or her to move about easily. The place where the leg has been amputated is very important. The more of the limb that is left, the more control the person will have over the artificial limb.

Prosthetic foot designs incorporate shock absorbers on the heel and instep to absorb the impact as the heel touches the ground and to allow a smooth "rollover" during walking. Recent designs based on carbon fiber springs are the most effective at storing and releasing energy during walking and, in particular, recreational and sports activities.

The knee joint is the most crucial part of a prosthetic leg. Until recently, thigh amputees have had to use prosthetic legs that lock straight during the weight-bearing part of walking, to prevent the leg from collapsing. This results in an unnatural gait and prevents any shock absorption. A growing number of prosthetic knee designs now include a "bouncy knee." As the amputee puts weight on the limb, a friction brake engages automatically and stabilizes the knee, while a small rubber element allows a few degrees of motion to absorb shock and simulate knee bending.

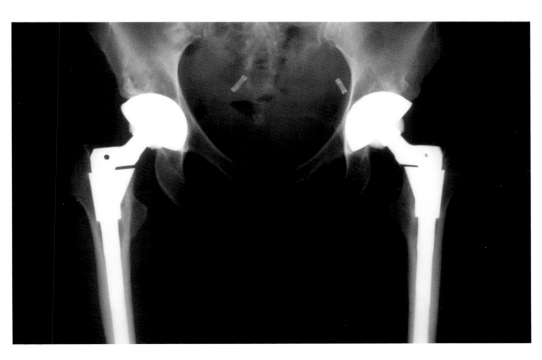

▶ *This X-ray photograph shows two prosthetic hip joints implanted in an elderly patient. Human joints deteriorate with age, and many elderly people need replacement hip joints. Prosthetic hips can last up to 30 years.*

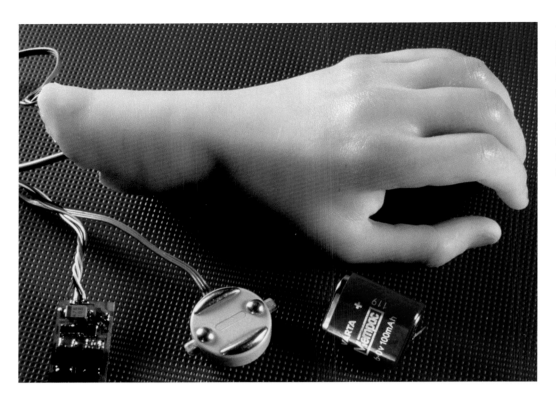

◄ *This modern prosthetic hand is made to look as lifelike as possible. The electrical contact on the wire detects nerve impulses in the person's arm. These electrical impulses, which are sent by the brain, can make the artificial hand move.*

Rather than using cumbersome belts and hinges, modern prosthetic legs may be attached by a cushioning sleeve that the amputee rolls onto the limb stump. A serrated pin at the end of the liner locks into the prosthesis. To remove the prosthesis, the amputee simply depresses a release button.

Hands and arms

Similar to prosthetic legs, prosthetic arms are still not perfect, but they are increasingly effective. Artificial hands, however, are far more difficult to make. Human hands are so complicated that it is impossible to make artificial ones that work as well.

Prosthetic arms and hands are often unpowered. When the patient has lost an arm above the elbow, a complicated system of straps and cables is often used. The patient is trained to make movements of the shoulder, the back, and the arm stump. These movements, by means of the straps and cables, allow the person to lock and unlock the artificial elbow joint, move the forearm up and down, and work the hand.

There is a great deal of research going on to improve artificial hands and arms. Some hands and arms have been designed that can be attached to the patient's existing muscles in such a way that movement of the prosthesis is controlled by the person's brain. The muscles are controlled by electrical signals from the brain. The brain can still transmit signals, even when a limb is no longer there. In one type of artificial hand, small electrical signals from the brain are sent to nerve endings in the muscle that remains. These tiny electrical signals are magnified and used to control the artificial hand. The person "thinks" the artificial hand to act in a certain way. After some practice, he or she can manage even quite delicate operations. Artificial hands of this kind can be powered by compressed gas or by electric motors.

The intelligent prosthesis

Most artificial limbs are "passive." They do not have any power of their own and cannot be moved of their own accord. This feature is common for two reasons. First, the power needed is so great that batteries would soon run down. Second, the electrical signals that control a person's muscles are weak. Only artificial hands can be easily powered because they need little power, and there are strong control signals from nerves in the forearm.

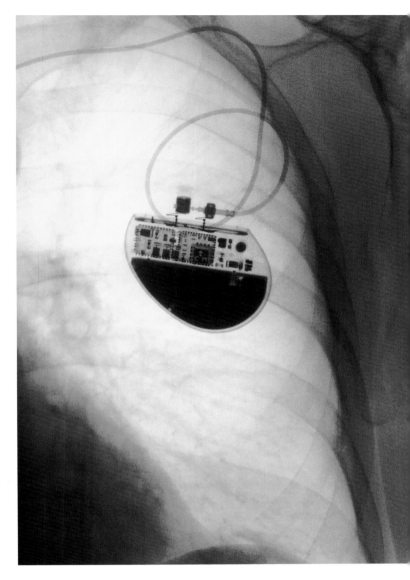

▶ **This X-ray image shows a person fitted with a pacemaker to regulate the heartbeat. Although it does not directly replace the heart, a pacemaker assists the heart's function and is classed as a prosthesis.**

In the early 1990s, "intelligent" prostheses were developed. These are not controlled by nerve signals but have sensors that continually assess the position of the limb in space. The data is fed into microprocessors, and the limb's freedom to move is adjusted according to the conditions detected. In "intelligent" legs, for example, hydraulic dampers in the knee are adjusted up to fifty times a second, optimizing knee stiffness throughout the walking cycle. This is a much greater level of control than can be achieved by unpowered mechanical legs and makes a great deal of difference, particularly when traversing uneven ground or walking down stairs.

New innovations for powering prostheses include the use of hydraulics (pressurized liquids). Hydraulics are used widely to power all sorts of machines, such as mechanical arms. Hydraulic systems use pistons connected to pipes containing high-pressure liquid. They are powerful and reliable, and they react very quickly. Electro-hydraulic systems maintain hydraulic pressure using an electric pump powered by batteries. More simple, heel-pump systems maintain pressure using a small pump built into the heel of the person's shoe. When he or she walks, liquid is forced up a tube to maintain the pressure in the system.

Artificial joints

One of the most common prosthetic operations, and one of the most successful, is hip-joint replacement. This operation becomes necessary when arthritis, or inflammation of the joint, begins to cause the person severe pain. A person who has a new hip joint is often changed from being an invalid to being an active person once more.

The materials used for the new joint must not be rejected by the patient's body, and they must not wear out over the years. After many years of research, it was found that the best results are achieved by a very smooth metal ball that fits into a plastic, cup-shaped socket. These two parts of the joint are fixed to the thigh bone and the hip bone using a special cement. Once fitted, these joints should last for at least thirty years. There are also operations to replace the knee joint, the elbow joint, and the small joints in the fingers.

A small number of patients are allergic to artificial joints. Their bodies try to reject the tiny particles of plastic and metal that are produced by the friction (rubbing) of the joint. For this reason, patients are usually tested before the operation to find out whether or not they are allergic to the materials in the prosthesis.

See also: HYDRAULICS • NERVOUS SYSTEM

Protein

Most people think of protein as something they must eat to stay healthy. Though this is true, there are also proteins within the body that do not come from food. Proteins help living cells grow and function properly. In fact, proteins are an essential part of all living things, whether they are a single-celled bacterium or a complex animal such as a human being.

Proteins are the building blocks of life (they make up about 50 percent of all living cells) and are fundamentally important to life. This importance was recognized by chemists in the early nineteenth century, who took the name for these substances from the Greek word *proteios*, meaning "primary."

There are thousands of different proteins in the body. Each has a unique structure and does a different job. Proteins, therefore, have a greater variety of chemical composition than any other compound in the human body. Structural proteins are essential to the growth and maintenance of plant and animal bodies and the walls of single cells. For example, they build, repair, and replace the body's tissues, muscles, and bones. Enzymes are proteins that are essential to nearly every chemical reaction that takes place in the body. Many hormones that act as chemical messengers are proteins. Transport proteins carry essential substances around the body, and antibodies are proteins that help fight infection.

▼ *The foods in this picture—meat, fish, eggs, milk, and cheese—all contain high levels of protein. Vegetables and other foods are generally much lower in protein, but good sources include nuts, peas, and beans.*

What is protein?

Proteins are produced in cells and are formed by chains of molecules called amino acids. The order of the amino acids in the chain makes the different proteins. There are more than 20 amino acids that occur naturally in proteins. While most of these amino acids are required by all organisms, the proteins of one species differ from those of another.

Amino acids are made up of atoms of carbon, hydrogen, oxygen, nitrogen, and sometimes sulfur. Amino acids are linked by peptide bonds to form what is called a polypeptide chain. A peptide bond is a link between the amino group ($-NH_2$) of one amino acid and the carboxyl group ($-COOH$) of another. The order of amino acids in the chain is called the primary structure of the protein. The chain may link up with another chain alongside it, or it may coil around itself. This linking or coiling is called the secondary structure. A further structure has to do with the three-dimensional shape of the protein, called the tertiary structure. Some proteins are entwined so that they appear to be knotted, while others look much less twisted.

Getting amino acids

Plants can make all the amino acids they need themselves. Animals, however, must obtain some of their amino acids from proteins from outside sources. In humans, eight amino acids must be taken in through food. These are called the "essential amino acids."

The levels of proteins in most plants are low, so animals such as ruminants (cows, for example), which only eat plants, require very large amounts of plant material to get the amino acids they need. Nonruminant animals (including humans) can

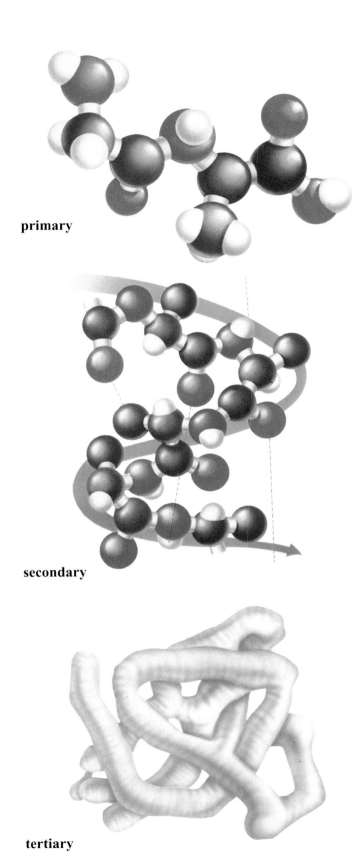

primary

secondary

tertiary

◀ *These illustrations show the different structures of proteins. First is the primary structure, which is one or more chains of amino acid molecules. The protein in this illustration consists of two amino acids. The black spheres are carbon atoms; the white are hydrogen; the red are oxygen; and the blue are nitrogen. The secondary structure can be the linking of chains around themselves. This protein has taken a coiled shape. The tertiary structure is the three-dimensional shape of the protein. This protein is so entwined that it looks knotted.*

more easily obtain proteins from animals and their products—meat, milk, eggs, and cheese, for example. They may also get proteins from a few rich plant sources of proteins. These include legumes (peas and beans) and cereal grains. Soybeans, which are the best vegetable source of proteins, are the basis of many foods eaten by human vegetarians and vegans.

In the human body, cells absorb (take in) amino acids from the duodenum, which is the first part of the small intestine. When a protein food, such as meat, enters the stomach, stomach acids start breaking the meat down into individual molecules of protein. These molecules then pass into the duodenum, and there the process of digestion breaks them down further into individual amino acids. The amino acids are then absorbed through the wall of the intestine and pass from there to the liver and into the bloodstream.

▼ *The photograph below shows red blood cells. They contain the protein hemoglobin, which acts as an oxygen carrier in the blood. In its oxygenated state, hemoglobin is bright red. When deoxygenated, it is purple-blue.*

Unlike carbohydrates and fats, proteins cannot be stored in the body for future use, so the cells must work all the time to produce them. Children, who grow at a fast rate, therefore need more protein than adults. For example, a baby under six months old needs about 3 ounces (2 grams) of protein for every 2 pounds (about 1 kilogram) of its body weight each day. An adult requires only half as much. Like children, adults who do not get enough protein will suffer from weak and useless muscles.

Sometimes people's bodies cannot make enough of the necessary proteins, and then the person may become ill. For example, insulin is a protein that is also a hormone. A lack of insulin causes a disease called diabetes.

Many jobs

One of the most important jobs of proteins is to build and rebuild tissue. The protein that does this is collagen. It makes up both the tissues themselves and the connective tissue that holds the various organs in place. Actin and myosin are muscle proteins. They produce the rapid contraction

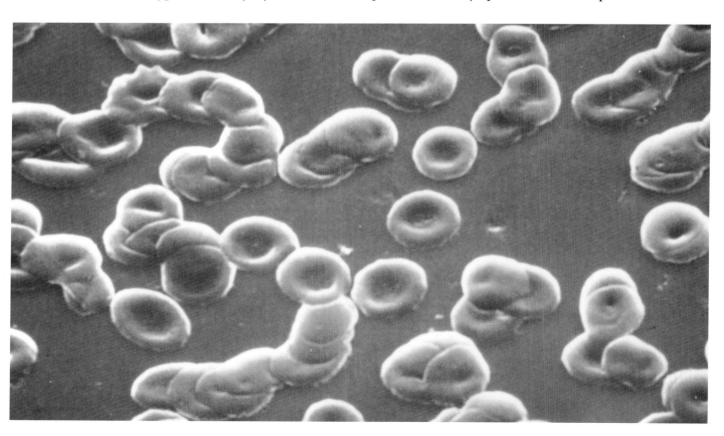

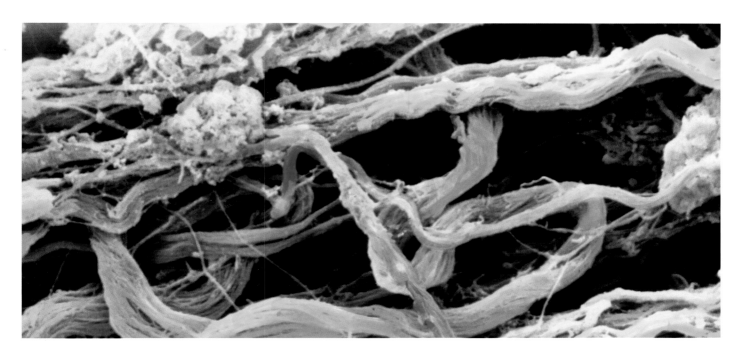

▲ *This colored electron micrograph shows bundles of collagen and elastin fibers in human connective tissue. Connective tissues are made from proteins and hold body organs in place. Collagen fibers are tough and inextensible (do not stretch), while elastin fibers have elastic properties.*

(tightening) and relaxation (loosening) that allows the body to move. Actin and myosin do this by forming a strong, interlocking molecular network.

All the known enzymes are proteins. Their main job is to act as catalysts (substances that speed up or initialize reactions) in the huge number of chemical reactions that keep the body working smoothly. An enzyme called pepsin acts on other proteins to help them work. Lipase enzymes act on fats, maltase on sugars, and amylase on starches.

Several hormones are proteins. Hormones have important regulatory functions in the body, controlling, for example, the rate of metabolism and the production of digestive enzymes. Insulin regulates carbohydrate metabolism by controlling glucose levels in the blood. Thyroglobulin regulates overall metabolism. Angiogenin induces the growth of blood vessels in tissues.

Some proteins dissolve in blood and circulate in the bloodstream. Their job is to keep the liquid blood from leaking into the tissues. Globulin, which is one of these blood proteins, also holds the antibodies that fight infection. Hemoglobin is another protein in the blood. It carries oxygen through the circulatory system. Albumin makes up about 50 percent of all the proteins in blood plasma. It helps move various substances around within the bloodstream. Albumin also helps direct the water in the body. In case of shock, an injection of albumin into the blood can help to restore the correct amount of fluid in the body and so help the heart keep up its normal function.

Nonfood proteins

Nonfood proteins in the body inlude keratin, which is responsible for forming hair, nails, and the horns of animals. Animal fur and wool, therefore, contain proteins. Some proteins are used for wider purposes. It has been found that adding enzymes to detergents makes them work better. Enzymes are also used to fix dyes and to refine sugar. They also play a role in the production of alcoholic drinks by helping to bring about fermentation and are also necessary for baking.

See also: AMINO ACID • CELL • DIGESTIVE SYSTEM • ENZYME • IMMUNE SYSTEM

Protist kingdom

The protist kingdom is a large group of single-celled organisms that includes algae, amoebas, and yeasts. Protists are too small to be seen with the naked eye, so biologists use microscopes to observe and study them. Protists are different than plants and animals, but they may survive in similar ways.

Until microscopes were invented, people thought that the living world could be divided into two groups, or kingdoms, called the plant kingdom and animal kingdom. Plants and animals have several obvious differences that made it easy to put species in the right kingdom. Plants are green, they are rooted to the ground, and they do not need to eat because they make their own food using the energy from sunlight and nutrients absorbed through the roots. Animals are different. They come in various colors, they can move around, and they need to eat food to survive.

Microscopic world

This simple view of the natural world changed when people began to study cells—the tiny units that make up the bodies of all living things. In the 1670s, Dutch naturalist Antoni van Leeuwenhoek (1632–1723) began to study tiny objects with a powerful lens. His lens was the first microscope, and he used it to look at animal and plant cells. He also saw many tiny life-forms that looked like cells living on their own. He called these creatures "animalcules." Most scientists agreed with van Leeuwenhoek that these organisms were simple animals and plants. The ones that could move around were called protozoans, which means "first animals." The green-celled organisms were thought to be plants and were called algae. Protozoans were included in the animal kingdom, and algae were grouped in the plant kingdom. When the fungi kingdom was introduced to classify organisms such as mushrooms and molds, single-celled organisms that resembled larger fungi were also included in the plant kingdom.

Cell types

As biologists studied more of the microscopic world, they discovered that many single-celled organisms were really very different from multicellular plants and animals, and from each other. (Multicellular organisms are those with bodies made from more than one cell.)

In 1960, biologists suggested that the way in which the living world was organized should be rearranged. They proposed dividing living organisms into two superkingdoms, called the prokaryotes and eukaryotes. Prokaryotes include the tiniest single-celled organisms that have a simple internal structure. Bacteria and certain algae were included in the prokaryote superkingdom.

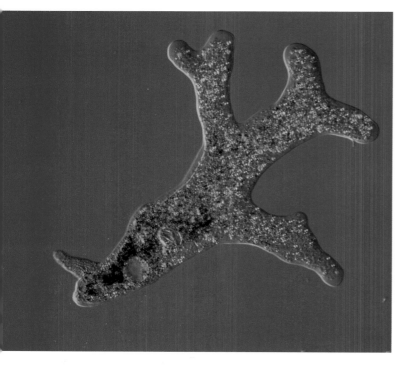

◄ *This magnified photograph shows a protist called* **Amoeba proteus.** *This animal-like protist is often called the giant amoeba because it is very large compared to most other amoebas.*

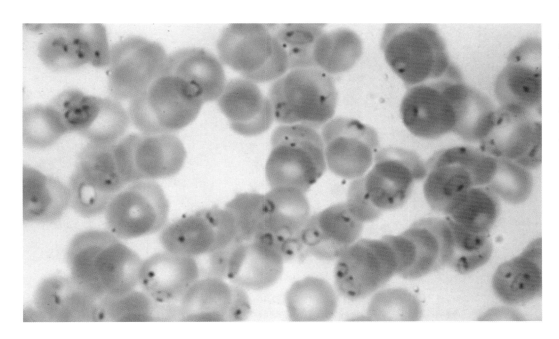

◄ *This magnified image shows* **Plasmodium falciparum** *parasites in human red blood cells.* **Plasmodium** *protists are responsible for malaria, which kills millions of people every year.*

All other organisms belong to the eukaryote superkingdom. Eukaryotes have large cells with complex internal structures called organelles. The eukaryotes were then divided up into four kingdoms—plants, animals, fungi, and a new group called the protists. The protist kingdom contains all eukaryotes that have just one cell.

Similar but different

Many protists share similarities with multicellular organisms, and it is likely that members of the plant, animal, and fungi kingdoms each evolved from single-celled, protistlike organisms. However, there are many more groups of protists that share some similarities with both plants and animals. For example, some types of algae can move. Therefore, although some protists are closely related to plants or animals, others are not closely related at all. Some biologists think that the protist kingdom really should be broken up into 30 smaller kingdoms. This would reflect the way in which many groups of protists are as different from each other as they are from plants, animals, and fungi.

Types of protists

Protists range in size from ⅟₅₀₀ inch (5 micrometers) to ⅟₁₀ inch (3 millimeters). Many protists group together into mats or clumps that can reach a large size. For example, brown algae may spread out into a thin sheet measuring almost 200 feet (60 meters) across. As a general rule, however, all the cells in these masses are structured in the same way, and they can survive on their own. Therefore, the cell masses are not considered to be a single organism. By contrast, the cells of plants and animals are all specialized to do many different jobs and cannot survive without each other.

DID YOU KNOW?

Many of the world's worst diseases are caused by protists that infect the human body. For example, malaria kills more than two million people every year, and another 250 million people suffer from it. Malaria is caused by a protist called *Plasmodium*, which passes into a person's blood when he or she is bitten by certain mosquitoes. Other diseases caused by protists include sleeping sickness, leishmaniasis, and some types of diarrhea. Sleeping sickness puts people into comas. It is caused by protists called trypanosomes, which are spread by the tsetse fly in Africa. Leishmaniasis is spread by infected sandflies.

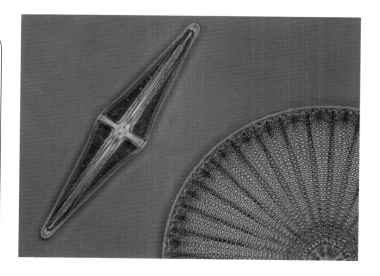

▲ *Diatoms are microscopic single-celled algae that contain the green pigment chlorophyll, which helps them absorb energy from sunlight. Diatoms form intricate glassy shells by absorbing dissolved silica from the waters in which they are found.*

Most protists live in water—even the thin layers of moisture on solid surfaces. However, many can survive out of water by forming hard cases, called cysts or tests, which protect them from drying out.

Complex structures

Protist cells are very complex because each one must carry out all the tasks needed to stay alive. The structure of the cells is extremely varied—some are surrounded by thick walls, while others are just fluid-filled sacs. Many protist cells have light-sensitive spots inside them, so they can move toward sources of light and heat.

A motile protist cannot rely on muscles to move about. Instead it uses cellular structures. Flagellates are a group of protists equipped with one or two tail-like flagella (*singular,* flagellum). Each flagellum can be waved like a whip, and this pushes the cell along.

Ciliates move using cilia (*singular,* cilium). Cilia are smaller than flagella and resemble tiny hairs. They line a large part of the cell surface. The cilia can be wafted in waves to push the protist along. The cilia may also be used to carry objects along the outside of the cell.

Amoebas move in a very different way. They extend part of their cell to form a structure called a pseudopodium (false foot). The rest of the cell contents then flows into the extension, and in this way the amoeba slides along.

Making their mark

Other protists include algae called diatoms and dinoflagellates. In the right conditions, these protists cause the blooms that sometimes color the ocean or river mouths. Diatoms also form glassy shells from silicates and other minerals from the sea. More animal-like organisms called radiolarians and foraminiferans live in huge numbers in seawater. When they die, the protists' tests sink to the seabed, forming a fine ooze. Over millions of years, the ooze turns into rocks, such as chalk and chert. Fungus-like protists called slime molds are bizarre organisms. Slime molds live as independent organisms when abundant nutrients are available but mass together and move as a group when they need to find a new source of nutrition.

See also: BACTERIA • FERMENTATION • FUNGI KINGDOM • YEAST

Psychiatry

The word *psychiatry* comes from the Greek words *psyche*, meaning "mind," and *iatreia*, which means "art of healing." Psychiatry is a branch of medicine that deals with the diagnosis, treatment, and prevention of all kinds of mental disorders. Psychiatrists work closely with clinical psychologists and social workers to diagnose mental disorders and provide treatment, usually by talking through a person's problems. Psychiatrists can also prescribe drugs to treat the problem.

▲ *Austrian psychiatrist Sigmund Freud is best known for his method of psychoanalysis to treat mental illness. He is also famous for his work on the interpretations of dreams and for his theories on sexuality.*

For thousands of years, most people with mental problems were kept locked up in asylums and were treated with cruelty. Mental illness was often viewed as a demonic possession, and it was not until the nineteenth century that it came to be seen as a medical problem. The origins of psychiatry lie with the efforts of French physician Philippe Pinel (1745–1826) and English physician J. Connolly, who both championed a sympathetic approach to the treatment of mental disorders.

The main tool of psychiatry is, simply enough, talking about the problem. All physicians must discuss a patient's symptoms and past medical history. Psychiatrists delve very deeply into everything that might have something to do with a person's mental state, including family life, likes and dislikes, school or working life, fears and pleasures, physical health, and many other feelings and emotions. The psychiatrist uses all this information to diagnose the problem and decide on the best course of treatment.

Many mental health problems are accompanied by a range of physical symptoms. For example, someone suffering from depression usually looks droopy, speaks very slowly, and does not blink very often. Someone who is anxious may fidget all the time, have sweaty palms, and sit on the edge of his or her chair. Someone who hears mysterious voices may often pause to listen. These physical symptoms can help the psychiatrist decide what kind of treatment is needed.

Psychotherapy is the main course of treatment for most mental problems. It is based on thorough discussion, often over many years, of the problems that might have caused the mental breakdown. The aim of psychotherapy is to help people understand the reasons behind their problems and build up their ability to handle them better.

► *A woman lies on a couch during a psychotherapy session. Freud pioneered psychoanalysis in the late nineteenth century, and it remains one of the most popular ways to treat mental illness.*

Freud and psychoanalysis

Psychotherapy can take several forms, one of which is psychoanalysis. Several people are recognized as important figures in the development of psychoanalysis, but most of the credit is given to Austrian neurologist Sigmund Freud (1856–1939).

At the turn of the last century, Freud published a number of scientific papers in which he outlined the methods of psychoanalysis. Freud believed that past experiences, especially events that occurred during childhood, shape the way a person reacts to events in the present and future. Freud also believed that the way people act and think consciously is affected by unconscious feelings and thoughts. Freud and his followers tried to bring these feelings and thoughts out of the unconscious so that his patients would see and understand the cause of their problems. In this way, psychoanalysis became a way for people to become less unhappy and adjust to their daily lives.

Different kinds of therapy

Freud's theories persist, even though many of them have been modified or, in some cases, discredited. Psychoanalysis continues to be an important part of modern psychiatry. During psychoanalysis, the person being analyzed relaxes on a couch and talks about anything that comes to mind. This is called free association. There is also discussion of dreams, considered a key to the unconscious part of the mind. From this informal discussion, the therapist tries to figure out what kinds of unconscious forces might be contributing to the problem.

Another form of psychotherapy is play therapy, in which troubled children act out their problems using toys and games. This is similar to psychodrama, in which adults act out roles in plays based on their problems.

Other treatments in psychiatry include medicinal drugs (pharmaceuticals), behavior therapy, and electroconvulsive therapy (ECT, sometimes called shock treatment). Pharmaceuticals are mainly used to calm, cheer up, or relax people. Behavior therapy uses a system of rewards and punishments to make people change the way they behave. ECT sends a mild electric current through the brain. It is a very strong treatment and should only be used when other forms of treatment have proved unsuccessful.

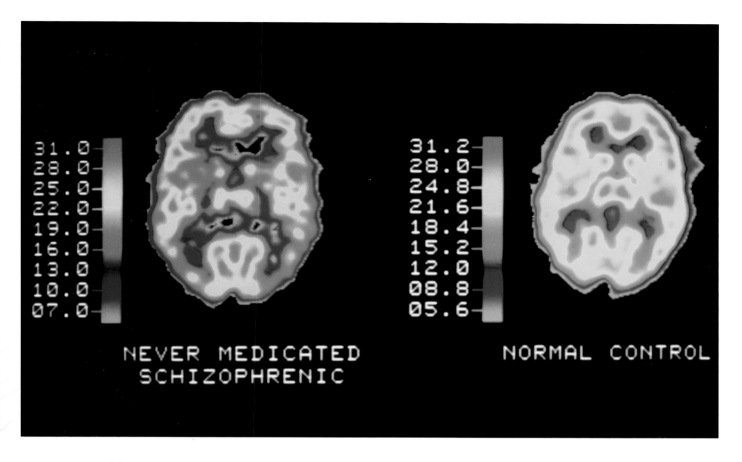

NEVER MEDICATED
SCHIZOPHRENIC

NORMAL CONTROL

▲ *Positron emission tomography (PET) scans show an axial section through a normal brain (right) and the brain of a schizophrenic. Red shows area of high activity, and blue or purple areas of low activity. The schizophrenic brain shows a distinctive pattern.*

Modern psychiatry

Psychiatry has changed a great deal. There are new medicines and treatments. Physicians now realize that some diseases of the body are caused by mental problems. They treat a person's body and mind together, rather than separately.

An example of a disease caused by mental illness is bulimia nervosa. This condition consists of regular periods of overeating followed by drastic attempts to lose weight, for example, by vomiting. Another example is post-traumatic stress disorder (PTSD). PTSD can follow any extremely distressing event. It affects hostages, or those involved in very stressful situations, such as rape, torture, or war. Sufferers can relive the experience, may become irritable and wary of others, and may lack concentration.

Another disease now being recognized is chronic fatigue syndrome (CFS), in which sufferers feel tired despite being otherwise healthy. One of the big problems with this sort of disease is convincing patients that they have a mental illness.

DID YOU KNOW?

Sigmund Freud was born on May 6, 1856, in Freiburg, in what is now the Czech Republic. When he was four years old, the family moved to Vienna, Austria. At age 17, Freud studied medicine at Vienna University, graduating in 1881. He returned to Vienna in 1886 to practice as a neurologist. When Freud published his psychoanalysis theory, he was ridiculed by his contemporaries. His theory was eventually recognized, and Freud was elected a member of the Royal Society, London, in 1936. In 1938, German forces invaded Austria, and Freud fled to London, where he died one year later.

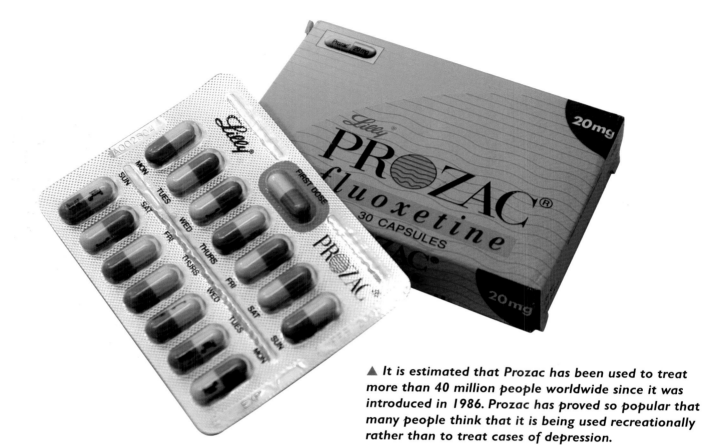

▲ **It is estimated that Prozac has been used to treat more than 40 million people worldwide since it was introduced in 1986. Prozac has proved so popular that many people think that it is being used recreationally rather than to treat cases of depression.**

Modern treatment methods

Once a psychiatrist diagnoses a mental disorder, he or she can then decide on the best course of treatment. In the case of CFS, patients actually need to exercise. People with CFS usually avoid exercise, because it makes them feel worse. Mental effort is needed before any improvement is possible. With the help of a therapist and a sympathetic family member, people with CFS can overcome the mental block to exercise and can then slowly recover.

In the late twentieth century, new pharmaceuticals were developed that helped people overcome depression with few side effects. Called selective serotonin reuptake inhibitors (SSRIs), these work by acting on a neurotransmitter (chemical messenger) in the brain, called serotonin. Such SSRIs include fluvoxamine, flupenthizol, and fluoxetine, marketed as Prozac in the United States beginning in 1987. Prozac proved very popular because people did not experience the same unpleasant side effects, such as anxiety and nausea,

that were associated with the tricyclic antidepressants. However, the widespread prescription of Prozac has proved controversial. There have been reports of people becoming aggressive and suicidal while taking the drug. It has also been suggested that people who are not clinically depressed are taking Prozac recreationally to enhance their mood.

Antidepressants can also help treat another common but often unrecognized condition, called obsessive-compulsive disorder (OCD). A typical example of OCD is the need for constant hand washing. A modern variant is computer hacking. In 1993, a young British hacker was tried for illegally accessing computer systems in several countries, including a cancer research institute. The man was acquitted, partly because of evidence that he was obsessed and could not prevent his actions, although he knew they were wrong.

See also: BRAIN • PSYCHOLOGY

Psychology

When scientists test the behavior of a rat running around in a maze, they are studying how the mind of the rat works to make it behave as it does. Psychology is the science that explores everything to do with the minds of humans and other animals. Psychologists use what they learn to interpret behavior, as well as to change and control it.

Psychology is the study of human and animal behavior. People have always wanted to know exactly how the mind works. Ancient Greek philosophers, such as Plato (c. 428–348 BCE) and Aristotle (384–322 BCE), theorized about the link between the brain and mind. The same theories were tested much later, most notably by French mathematician and philosopher René Descartes (1596–1650), who put forward his famous philosophical argument *Cogito ergo sum* ("I think, therefore I am"). Psychology developed into a distinct science at the end of the nineteenth century

◀ *A rat finds some cheese in a complex maze. U.S. psychologist Edward C. Tolman (1886–1959) used mazes to test the theory of cognitive learning. After his rats had run the maze and reached the food reward, Tolman altered the maze to allow for a short cut to the food. The greatest number of rats chose the short cut to the food. Tolman suggested that the rats had not learned a fixed path to reach the food but had a cognitive knowledge of the location of the food.*

thoughts and feelings under controlled conditions. This was the first time rigorous scientific methods had been applied to the study of mental processes. In 1881, Wundt launched the first journal of psychology. In recognition of his enormous contribution, Wundt is often called the founding father of modern psychology.

The third major breakthrough was made by U.S. psychologist William James (1842–1910). In 1875, James set up his own psychology laboratory at Harvard University. James pioneered the principles of psychophysics, aiming to study the effects of physical processes on the mind of an organism. James's work culminated in the publication of *Principles of Psychology* (1890), a landmark psychology text published in two huge volumes.

Schools of thought

The first psychologists were either structuralists or functionalists. Structuralists believed that the main purpose of psychology is to describe and define what people see and hear through their senses. Functionalists were interested in what the mind could accomplish through its mental processes.

Behaviorism was introduced in 1913 by U.S. psychologist John Broadus Watson (1878–1958), a professor at Johns Hopkins University in Baltimore, Maryland. Behaviorists study how people and animals react in certain situations and use the results to predict patterns of behavior.

Gestalt psychology grew out of opposition to behaviorism in the early twentieth century thanks in large part to the work of German psychologist Max Wertheimer (1880–1943). *Gestalt* is the German word for "form," and gestalt psychologists believe that people see things in patterns. They developed the famous inkblot test to study how people see whole forms rather than parts of things at a time.

The behaviorist approach dominated psychology until after World War II (1939–1945), when cognitive psychology became popular. The success of cognitive psychology owes much to the development of the computer. Cognitive psychologists test their theories using complex computer programs.

▲ *This photograph of Wilhelm Wundt was taken around 1910. Wundt is considered to be the founding father of modern psychology. In 1879, he established the first laboratory dedicated to experimental psychology.*

thanks to three major developments. The first came in 1874, when German philosopher Franz Brentano (1838–1917) published his book *Psychology from an Empirical Standpoint,* in which he tried to establish a scientific study of the mind. A year later, German physiologist and psychologist Wilhelm Wundt (1832–1920) set up the first psychology laboratory at the Leipzig University, Germany. Wundt championed experimental work using a process called introspection. In this process, he encouraged his subjects to observe and talk about their own

◄ *Preschool children play on a tire swing. Motor (movement) skills such as balancing, jumping, and running are all acquired in the preschool years.*

throughout the world. However, psychology is different from psychiatry, which is a branch of medicine that deals only with mental illnesses.

Educational psychology

Educational psychology deals with the learning process by pinpointing difficulties or problems some children face at school. There are many psychological tests used to measure intelligence and other skills. These tests can help psychologists make a diagnosis that will help a child with an unknown problem. For example, a child may fall behind other children in his or her class. A psychologist may learn through tests that the child suffers from dyslexia, which is a condition that makes it hard for a person to read. This condition has nothing to do with lack of intelligence.

Social psychology

Social psychology looks at the relationships between people. Social psychologists try to figure out how and why people form friendships with some people and have conflicts with others. Social psychologists are also interested in explaining the behavior of different classes and cultures.

Another example of the work of social psychologists is the study of how violence in society affects the way people think and act. Social psychologists also examine the effects of books, computer games, newspapers, and television.

Developmental psychology

Developmental psychologists study the changes in people from babyhood to old age. They can tell people what they can expect to happen at different periods of life, which may help them to be better prepared to understand these changes when they come. This might save them from becoming upset or worried. For example, teenage rebellion is a natural part of growing up. If parents try to understand this natural process, everyone in the family should be able to get along better.

They also rely on advanced imaging techniques to measure the electrical activity and blood flow through the brain during different behaviors.

Nowadays, psychologists use all or part of these various methods in their work.

MODERN PSYCHOLOGY

Contemporary psychologists look at every form of mental process and all kinds of experience. They study the senses and how they help people solve problems. Psychologists try to figure out the reasons for breakdowns in normal mental processes, how people think and feel, and what lies behind the needs or desires that cause people to take various actions. One of the most important aims of psychology is to teach people how to get along with each other—whether children and parents, people in the same society, or all peoples

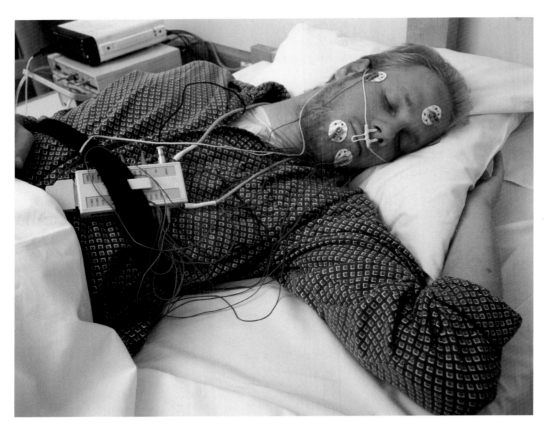

◄ *A man is monitored during sleep research at the Sleep Laboratory in Erasme Hospital, Brussels, Belgium. The electrodes attached to his face are linked to equipment that monitors brain activity. Analysis of sleep patterns is used in the study of sleeping disorders. It is also used to investigate the circadian (daily) rhythm, an internal biological clock that controls periods of wakefulness and sleep.*

Physiological psychology

Many people consider physiological psychology to be the most specialized branch of psychology. Physiological psychologists explore the physical base of the mind through the study of the brain. It is known that certain parts of the brain are related to certain thought processes. For example, there are tiny areas that control basic human motivations, such as hunger and thirst. Other tiny areas of the brain govern reactions such as anger and compassion. Some psychologists believe that parts of the brain may control even consciousness itself.

One question that physiological psychologists try to answer is how the brain cells can store the memory of a poem or a song, produce the emotion of anger or love, or control the activities people do without thinking about how they do them.

Industrial psychology

Industry needs managers and employees who get along with each other while doing their jobs in the best possible way. Industrial psychologists look for ways to make work relations better. They study how to avoid the stresses and irritations that could lead to conflicts between staff, and they try to show how to build trust between different workers.

Industrial psychology is also involved with the design of buildings and products. For example, the arrangement of the controls on the instrument panels of an airplane cockpit is based on psychologists' studies of how well people notice objects out of the corners of their eyes. The controls are also arranged and colored to help pilots concentrate over long periods of time.

Clinical psychology

Clinical psychologists usually work in schools and hospitals, dealing directly with children and patients who need their help. Like psychiatrists, they diagnose problems and give treatment, mostly by talking about what is troubling people. However, they do not usually prescribe drugs and must work with psychiatrists on any medical treatment.

See also: BRAIN • MEDICAL IMAGING • PSYCHIATRY

Pulley

A pulley is a device used for lifting heavy loads or driving machinery. It consists of a wheel with a rope, belt, or chain wrapped tightly around it. People have been using pulleys for thousands of years. Today, pulleys are used everywhere from building sites to automobile engines.

Although the pulley is simply a wheel with a groove in it for holding a cord, the idea for its use came much later in history than the wheel itself. The first evidence of a pulley is found in a sculpture from Mesopotamia (now Iraq) dating back about 2,800 years ago. A real pulley of a slightly later date was found in the ruins of ancient Calah (now Nimrud) in the same area. These ancient pulleys were probably used to raise water from wells or to hoist masts for shipbuilding.

Lifting pulleys

The simplest kind of pulley is the type commonly used on a building site for lifting heavy loads. The rim of a lifting pulley's wheel has a groove in it, and a rope fits into the groove. The load is attached to one end of the rope, and the other end of the rope hangs freely. If someone applies effort by pulling on the free end of the rope, the load can be raised.

It is much easier to pull down than to pull up. So it is much easier for someone to use a pulley to lift a heavy weight than to try to lift it themselves. A pulley changes the direction of the force being applied and makes it possible to use the person's own weight as part of that force.

Block and tackle

If a person wanted to lift a weight as heavy as him- or herself, he or she could probably do it with a single pulley. If a load is heavier than the person wanting to lift it, however, he or she would need

▲ This huge block-and-tackle pulley system is being used on a drilling rig. Block-and-tackle pulley systems can make it much easier to lift heavy equipment, such as these drilling pipes.

more help. The best way of increasing the pulling force is to put several pulleys together in a system called a block and tackle, which has two sets of pulleys. Each set is on a shaft and enclosed in a frame. The top set is fixed. The lower set is movable and has a hook attached to it from which to hang the load. A rope runs around each pulley in turn, with the load attached to a part of the block and tackle.

To lift a load with a block and tackle, the load is hooked onto the movable part, and the other end of the rope is pulled. It takes much less effort than lifting a load with a single pulley, because a single pulley has only one piece of rope to take the weight of the load. In a three-pulley system, for example, there are three sections of rope going from the lower to the upper part and thus pulling upward on the load. In a four-pulley system, there are four sections of rope, and so on. So, in theory, each

▶ *These illustrations show three simple pulley arrangements—a single pulley, two-pulley, and three-pulley system. The greater the number of pulleys, the greater the load that can be lifted with the same effort.*

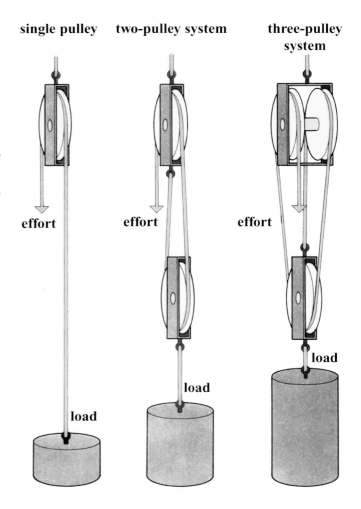

single pulley   two-pulley system   three-pulley system

effort   effort   effort

load   load   load

section of rope in a four-pulley system takes one-quarter of the load, and the tension (stress) throughout each section is equal to one-quarter of the weight of the load. Therefore, to raise a load using a four-pulley block and tackle, only one-quarter of the effort is needed, compared to that required to raise the same load with a single pulley. In other words, the pulley's force is multiplied by four.

In practice, however, the force is multiplied slightly less than the number of pulleys, because of the friction between the rope and wheels and the weight of the lower half of the block and tackle. The person pulling has to use extra force to overcome the effect of these two factors. The more pulleys there are, the greater the weight of the lower part and the more friction there is. When there are more than six pulleys, the friction and weight are too much for the block and tackle to work well. So the usual number of pulleys in a block-and-tackle system is four.

Driving mechanisms

The pulleys in the illustrations (above right) freewheel on their own shafts—they are not attached to anything. But this sort of pulley can also be used to drive a system such as a clock mechanism. A cord or chain with a weight on the end of it is attached to the pulley. As the weight travels downward, the pulley drives the clock. When the weight has gone down as far as it can, the clock is wound up by returning the weight to the top.

Drive pulleys

Drive pulleys work slightly differently from lifting pulleys. A belt, not a rope, connects two pulleys, each on its own shaft. The edges of the pulleys may be flat, or they may have a V-shaped groove to hold the belt. A V-shaped belt is better than a flat belt because it can be narrower but stronger and therefore can provide more power. When the drive

pulley is turned, power is sent through the belt to the second pulley. This type of pulley is used to power the fan belt of an automobile.

Smooth pulley belts can stretch and slip at high speeds, so another type of drive pulley uses a toothed belt. This interlocks with teeth on the pulleys, which are similar to gear wheels, making it possible to control the speed and timing of the pulley. Toothed drive pulleys are used to drive the camshafts of automobile engines.

The speed of the driven pulley depends on the size of the drive pulley. If both are the same size, they turn at the same speed. If the drive pulley is larger than the driven pulley, then the driven pulley turns faster. If the drive pulley is smaller than the driven pulley, the driven pulley turns more slowly.

See also: GEAR • WINCH AND WINDLASS

Pump

A pump is a machine for pushing a liquid or a gas from one place to another. Often it is used by farmers for raising water for their crops from below the ground or out of a river. This kind of pump is one of the oldest pieces of machinery that is still being used in the world today.

The invention of the pump was an answer to the great need to irrigate (supply water to) crops in the dry lands of the Middle East. For a long time, buckets of water had to be carried from the rivers to the fields, but this was slow, back-breaking work. The first pump appeared in Mesopotamia (now Iraq) about five thousand years ago. It was called a *shaduf*, and it was the only pump in use for more than two thousand years. In fact, it is still used in some countries of the Middle East and Africa today.

The *shaduf* comprises a long wooden pole attached to a pair of upright wooden posts with a pivot. A bucket is fastened to one end of the pole and a counterweight (an object of the same weight) attached to the other end. When the lever is pushed down, the bucket dips into the water source and fills. When the counterweight is pulled, the pole and bucket are easily raised. The bucket can then be swung around and the water poured into an irrigation channel, for example.

About 2,500 years later, other kinds of pumps came into use. One of these was the *saqiya*, which was a large wheel with a row of pots tied to the outer edge. As the wheel was turned, the lowest pots dipped into the water and filled. As the filled pots came to the top of the rotating wheel, they emptied into a chute leading to an irrigation canal. Later, the pots were replaced by troughs built into the wheel itself. Another type of early pump worked like the *saqiya*, but it had no wheel. Instead, buckets were attached to a continuous chain, which passed over a pulley to dip and raise the containers into and out of the water.

The most ingenious early pumps were based on the Archimedian screw, invented by ancient Greek mathematician and scientist Archimedes (c. 287–21 BCE). The Archimedian screw comprised a large

▶ *This engraving shows a reciprocating, positive displacement pump designed by John Keeling in London, England, around the time of the Great Fire of London in 1666. The development of pumps has been largely driven by the needs of firefighting.*

◄ *This photograph shows a simple hand pump being used to pump water from an underground well in Africa. Simple pumps such as these can make a huge difference to people in poor, arid areas of the world.*

Positive displacement pumps

The ancient Romans had a pump (now called the Bolsena pump, for the town in Italy where one was found) that had valves and a plunger. It was a positive displacement pump—that is, each stroke of the plunger displaced a fixed amount of water. Many modern pumps are of this type.

An example of a modern positive displacement pump is the bicycle pump. At each stroke, the plunger pushes the same amount of air into the tire. Like the Bolsena pump, it also has a nonreturn valve. A nonreturn valve will let fluid pass in one direction only. So, on the return stroke, the bicycle pump fills with air again.

Large reciprocating pumps (pumps that go in and out like the bicycle pump) were used in the eighteenth and nineteenth centuries for pumping water out of mines and maintaining the water level in canals. With some extra valves and seals, reciprocating pumps can be designed as double-action pumps. Double-action pumps push water or air out on both the in-stroke and the out-stroke.

Rotary pumps work in a different way from reciprocating pumps, although they, too, are positive displacement pumps. Rotary pumps have no valves and work by pushing the water continuously with turning blades from the inlet through to the outlet. The amount of fluid displaced depends on the volume between the blades. Gasoline pumps are of the rotary type.

Two types of positive displacement pumps can be used to pump liquids that are mixed with solids. Ordinary pumps can easily get clogged by solids. In

wooden pipe enclosing a long helix (spiral structure). The device was inclined at an angle of about 45 degrees to the horizontal, and its lower end dipped into the water. The device was then rotated. As the screw turned, it raised water inside the pipe and emptied it into a chute at the top. The Archimedian screw was in wide use throughout the Roman Empire about 2,100 years ago. Modern screw pumps are used for pumping sewage in wastewater treatment plants, because the design permits the passage of debris without clogging.

DID YOU KNOW?

Today, pumps are the second most common machines in use, after the electric motor. Pumps can be made of plastic, bronze, and even titanium.

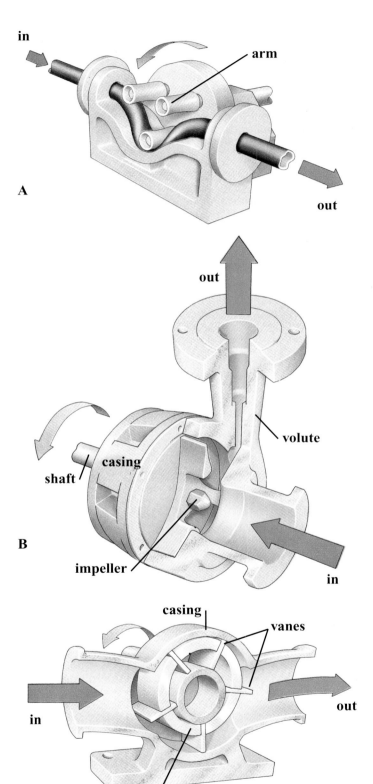

a diaphragm pump, however, the liquid and solids are kept away from the mechanism by a diaphragm. This is connected to a piston that pushes the diaphragm in and out to propel the liquid. The valves must be large enough not to be clogged by the solids, however.

The other type of pump that can move solids mixed with liquids is the peristaltic pump. This is a rotary pump and has no valves. Unlike the ordinary rotary pump, however, the mechanism does not come into contact with the liquid, which is held in a flexible tube. This tube is squeezed continuously by the rotary motion of the pump, similar to pushing water along a rubber tube by pressing a finger along the outside of it. This type of pump is used to move blood in a heart-lung machine.

Reciprocating pumps are commonly used for raising water. Fuel pumps in cars and trucks are usually of the diaphragm type. Hydraulic pumps for jacks, airplane controls, and earthmoving machinery are also positive displacement pumps.

Centrifugal pumps

The centrifugal pump was developed in the middle of the nineteenth century. Centrifugal force pushes outward from the middle of a rotating object. It is the force that keeps the water in a bucket when it is swung around fast enough at arm's length.

In the pump, fluid is fed into the center of a bladed wheel called an impeller, which is housed inside a case. As the impeller rotates at high speed, the fluid is forced outward through an outlet. If the

◄ *These illustrations show three of the most common types of positive displacement pumps. In the peristaltic or compressing pump (A), each of the three arms in turn squeezes liquid through the flexible tube. This works like the action of human intestines. In the centrifugal pump (B), the rotor is called an impeller. It impels (pushes) the fluid around the casing and applies a centrifugal force (a force pushing out from the center) to it. The upper casing, called the volute, has a tube that widens. This changes the fluid from a fast-moving, low-pressure flow to a slow-moving, high-pressure flow. In the rotary pump (C), the fluid is pushed straight through the casing by the spinning rotor. The vanes (blades) can be made of either rubber, plastic, or metal.*

◀ These centrifugal pumps are being used to pump water through a water treatment plant in Paris, France.

high speed of the fluid is reduced, the pressure is increased, and so the outlet tube generally becomes wider to slow the fluid down. This widening outlet is called the volute.

Other types of pumps

Some pumps are neither centrifugal nor positive displacement types. For example, the air ejector, or jet pump, is worked by air from a compressor. The jet of air passes across the outside of an opening in a chamber and creates a partial vacuum (airless space) inside the chamber, which can be used to pull liquid into the chamber.

The hydraulic ram is a specialized type of pump that raises water using water power itself. An airlift pump is a simple device that uses either gas or compressed air bubbles to raise liquids in a pipe.

Nuclear reactors use liquid metals, such as mercury, to transfer heat from one part of the reactor to another. These metals need to be pumped around, and for this purpose the electromagnetic pump has been designed. A constant magnetic field is passed through the liquid at right angles to the direction of the flow required in the pipe. The magnetic field pushes the liquid metal along in the same way as a direct current

(DC) electric motor is pushed around by a magnetic field. The electromagnetic pump has the advantage that the mercury can be kept apart from the pump in a separate tube.

Priming a pump

Some pumps can pump only liquids, not air, so when they are empty, these pumps must be primed—that is, have the process activated by pushing some liquid into them.

When the pump is above the level of the liquid, there will be air between it and the liquid it is to pump. An ordinary centrifugal pump will not pull the air from the suction pipe. A wet self-priming pump is widely used to avoid this difficulty. The body of the pump is filled with liquid, which cannot escape because of a nonreturn valve in the pump body. This liquid pushes the air from the suction pipe and allows the pump to raise the liquid. Sometimes a jet pump is used to help centrifugal pumps where the liquid is mixed with large quantities of air. The jet pump works equally well with air or a liquid, such as water.

See also: ARCHIMEDES • CENTRIFUGE • PRESSURE

Pythagoras

The most famous discovery of Greek scholar Pythagoras was the theorem stating that in a right-angled triangle, the square of the hypotenuse (the longest side) is equal to the sum of the squares of the other two sides. Pythagoras also provided a mathematical description of the musical scale and was the first person to make the connection between musical harmony and numbers.

The first Greek scholar to recognize that certain shapes have the same characteristics, whatever their size, was probably Thales of Miletus (625–547 BCE), who tried to establish the basics of geometry. Thales of Miletus would not have succeeded had it not been for Pythagoras, who is believed to have studied under him.

The traveler

Little is known about the early life of Pythagoras other than that he was born on the Greek island of Samos around 580 BCE. It is generally accepted that Pythagoras traveled extensively during his early years. Some attribute this to Thales, who may have told Pythagoras to broaden his knowledge of mathematics by travel. However, there is also a belief that Pythagoras was forced to flee Samos as a result of the island's tyrannical ruler, Polycrates. Whatever the reason, Pythagoras was clearly influenced by contemporary scholars in Asia Minor. He is said to have visited, among others, the priests of Zoroaster (the Magi), who were great mathematicians of the Persian empire.

The brotherhood

It is known that Pythagoras settled in Crotona in southern Italy, which was then part of the Greek empire, around 530 BCE. There, he founded a

▲ This bust of Pythagoras dates from around 530 BCE, shortly after the great philosopher and mathematician returned from his travels in Asia Minor.

religious and politically active community of aristocrats. The Pythagorean brotherhood was a success, making many important mathematical and philosophical discoveries. Pythagoras taught his disciples to worship numbers and to believe in reincarnation—that souls do not die but are born again in another human being or animal. He also insisted that his followers remain anonymous and use the name of the brotherhood on any of their writings or whenever they made discoveries.

Pythagoras's discoveries

Pythagoras is best remembered for his theorem about the lengths of sides in a right-angled triangle. The Babylonians had discovered the same idea one

▲ *Among the many mathematical investigations of the Pythagoreans were the studies of the properties of odd, even, prime, and square numbers. Many of their ideas are fundamental to basic math.*

thousand years before but had been unable to prove it. This theorem is still useful in science and also in everyday life. For example, an architect uses the theorem to ensure that the rooms in a new house are laid out in perfect rectangles.

Pythagorean ideas on numbers were partly mystical. His followers believed that nature somehow depended on numbers, and they sought a numerical description for all that they saw around them. One such idea was in their study of the harmonics of stringed instruments. They discovered that a vibrating string produces notes that lie at various harmonic intervals from one another. They thought these could all be shown to be ratios of two whole numbers (such as $\frac{5}{6}$ or $\frac{1}{2}$). They even believed that the orbits of the planets were a harmonic interval apart.

Unfortunately, this neat theory was shattered by the discovery of irrational numbers. These are numbers that cannot be expressed as a ratio of two whole numbers—such as the square root of 2, which is 1.41421. This new discovery so upset the Pythagorean brotherhood that its followers tried to keep it quiet. In fact, it was the first step in the development of a new and important branch of mathematics known as number theory.

The end of the Pythagoreans

The Pythagorean brotherhood was influential in the politics of Crotona, and some of these political ideas influenced several western Greek colonies. However, the Pythagorean brotherhood had many enemies and became unpopular. During one particular uprising in Crotona, many members of the Pythagorean brotherhood were killed. The others had to flee from persecution, and it is thought that Pythagoras escaped to Metapontum, where he died around 500 BCE. The Pythagorean brotherhood continued to teach for about fifty years after Pythagoras's death but eventually succumbed to continued suppression.

See also: MATHEMATICS • MUSICAL INSTRUMENT • NUMBER SYSTEM

Quantum theory

Quantum theory was developed in the early twentieth century because the long-accepted classical laws of physics could not explain the results scientists were getting from some of their experiments. The theory contained the new idea that energy consists of bundles or bursts called quanta (*singular,* quantum).

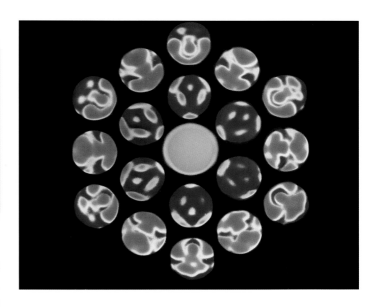

▲ *This photograph shows the electron diffraction pattern produced when a beam of electrons bounces off a crystal of an alloy of titanium and nickel. The electrons seem to act like light waves. Classical laws of physics cannot explain how electrons produce these distinctive diffraction patterns, but quantum theory does account for the wave nature of electrons.*

By the end of the nineteenth century, scientists felt that the laws of physics were complete. English physicist and mathematician Isaac Newton (1642–1727) had formulated the laws of motion to describe the behavior of everything from planets to people. There were also laws to explain magnetism and electricity and all forms of radiation, such as heat, visible light, and X-rays.

However, some observations could not be explained using the classical laws. For example, physicists had been studying the radiation emitted by objects called blackbodies. An example of a blackbody at low temperatures is the pupil of the eye, which appears black because any light energy that falls on it is absorbed in the eye. Blackbodies also emit energy at any temperature more efficiently than any other bodies at the same temperature. However, the physicists found that the distribution of energy among the different wavelengths emitted by a blackbody could not be explained by the classical laws of physics.

Planck's ideas

In 1900, German physicist Max Planck (1858–1947) came up with an answer. Planck was describing the behavior of a blackbody when it was heated. Planck reasoned that the old laws did not apply because scientists assumed that energy radiated from a body in a continuous (unbroken) flow. Planck suggested that the energy could enter or leave the body only in tiny bundles, called quanta. The size of the energy bundle depended on the frequency of the light, according to the equation:

$$E = h\nu$$

where E is the energy of the quantum, ν is the frequency of the light, and h is Planck's constant (measured as 6.6×10^{-34} joules per second).

Planck published his work without understanding the full meaning of his assumption about energy quanta. Indeed, it took another five years before German-born U.S. physicist Albert Einstein (1879–1955) came up with an explanation for Planck's results.

Einstein and the photoelectric effect

In 1905, Einstein published four academic papers that revolutionized the scientific world. One of these papers concerned the nature of light. In his

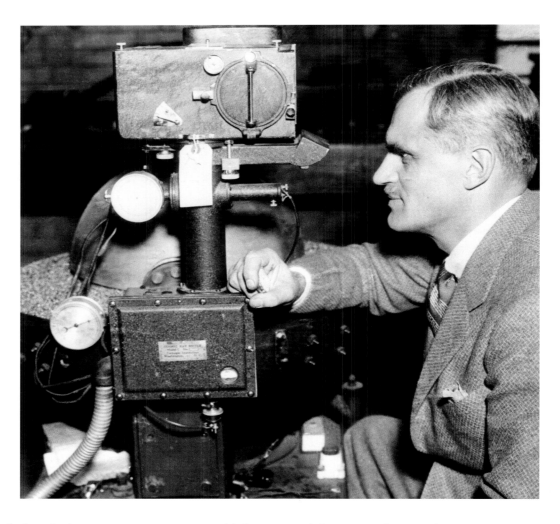

▶ *U.S. physicist Arthur Holly Compton provided convincing experimental evidence that light exists as particles of radiant energy, called quanta. Conducted in 1923, his experiment showed that photons (light particles) collide with electrons in a way that is similar to a collision between two billiard balls.*

paper, Einstein suggested that light is not a wave but a particle—a tiny bundle of energy called a photon. Furthermore, Einstein suggested that photons could not be divided into smaller particles and that they were the basic unit of energy. Einstein then used his idea of the photon to explain the results of Planck's blackbody experiments and, most notably, the photoelectric effect.

In the late nineteenth century, scientists had found that light could eject electrons from a metal in a process called the photoelectric effect. According to the laws of classical physics, the amount of light falling on the metal should determine how many electrons would be ejected from the metal. However, scientists found that the frequency of the light was the critical factor. No amount of light below a certain frequency would eject electrons from the metal. Einstein explained this irregularity by suggesting that each electron

could be ejected by one photon, but only if the photon had enough energy and therefore a high enough frequency (remember that energy and frequency are related by Planck's equation).

Einstein is best remembered for his theories of special and general relativity. Nevertheless, Einstein won the 1921 Nobel Prize for physics for his paper on the photoelectric effect.

The Compton effect

The mounting body of evidence in support of quantum theory did not convince all of the scientific community. Many scientists continued to grasp onto the classical laws of physics, even though it was clearly apparent that classical physics did not hold all the answers to all the questions.

In 1923, however, U.S. physicist Arthur Holly Compton (1892–1962) performed an experiment that helped sway support in favor of Einstein's idea of the photon. Compton beamed high-frequency light through different substances and noted that the light scattered as it passed through. When Compton measured the frequency of the scattered light, he noted that the frequency was lower than that of the original light. Compton suggested that photons collide with electrons inside the atoms of the substance. During the collision, the photon loses energy to the electron according to the laws of conservation of energy and momentum. As a result, the scattered light Compton observed was of a lower frequency than the original light. This is called the Compton effect.

Wave or particle?

For hundreds of years, scientists have been arguing about whether light consists of waves or particles. From experimental evidence, scientists know light behaves in a way similar to a ripple spreading on the surface of a pond. Where waves overlap, they either reinforce each other or cancel each other out. This is called interference. One can see the effects of interference in the colors of oil on a wet road.

At the same time, modern light detectors can detect the individual photons from light sources, so scientists now agree that light behaves both as waves and as particles.

The wave-particle duality of light was subject to much debate in the 1920s, but the scientific community gradually accepted the idea. In 1923, however, French physicist Louis-Victor-Pierre-Raymond de Broglie (1892–1987) added to the controversy by suggesting that all matter behaves as both particles and waves. Experimental evidence confirmed the wave nature of matter in 1927.

Quantum mechanics

The work of de Broglie laid the foundations for a mathematical description of quantum theory, called quantum mechanics. Austrian physicist

▶ *Austrian physicist Erwin Schrödinger developed an equation that describes the wavelike behavior of subatomic particles. This equation is the fundamental law of quantum theory. Schrödinger was awarded the 1933 Nobel Prize for physics in honor of his work.*

DID YOU KNOW?

One effect of quantum physics is now being tested. In 1935, Schrödinger described a "thought experiment" that no one would ever do. Suppose one puts a cat in a box fitted with a device that gives a 50 percent chance of killing the cat in an hour. Quantum theory describes the state of the cat as being a combination of living and dead. This is so out of line with human experience that many physicists felt something must be wrong. Physicists are still experimenting, but they are not using a cat. Instead, they are using superconducting quantum interference devices (SQUIDs) to figure out more about the curious world of quantum theory.

▲ *Scientists work on the alpha magnetic spectrometer (AMS) detector, which is a particle physics experiment destined for the International Space Station and designed to detect antimatter in space. The existence of antimatter was born out of the relativistic quantum theory developed by British scientist Paul Dirac in 1927.*

Erwin Schrödinger (1887–1961) formulated the central equation of quantum mechanics, called the Schrödinger equation, in 1926. It is testament to Schrödinger's exceptional talent that this equation remains central to the ideas of quantum theory.

The uncertainty principle

In 1927, German physicist Werner Karl Heisenberg (1901–1976) published his uncertainty principle, which states that it is impossible to know exactly where a particle is and how fast it is moving at the same time. Heisenberg's uncertainty principle is a challenging concept. Effectively, it states that it is impossible to describe accurately events in the natural world. As such, it broke the long-standing laws of classical physics that the natural world was infinitely measurable and therefore predictable.

DID YOU KNOW?

In 1989, a group of Japanese physicists sent a beam of electrons through a pair of narrow slits to observe the interference caused by the wavelike properties of electrons. With one hundred electrons, they finished up in random positions. With large numbers of electrons, however, they saw an interference pattern of light and dark bands typical of waves. In the early 1990s, scientists in the United States and Germany observed similar effects with beams of helium and sodium atoms. This proves that solid matter can behave like waves. The techniques are providing a useful way of testing quantum theory.

See also: ATOM AND MOLECULE • BOHR, NIELS • EINSTEIN, ALBERT • ELECTRICITY • MAGNETISM • PHYSICS • PLANCK, MAX

Radar

If a flashlight is shone at a wall, the light beam bounces off the surface of the wall and back toward the source. Similarly, an echo may be heard if someone claps his or her hands in front of a cliff. Radio waves behave in the same way. When beamed by a radio transmitter, they will bounce off any objects in their path. In radar, reflected radio waves are used to reveal the exact position of an object.

Very early in the study of radio waves, scientists came up with the idea of making a device to "see" at a distance by means of radio waves reflected off the surface of the faraway object. The device invented was called radar—short for "radio detection and ranging." Radar allows distant objects to be detected even in fog and at night and gives both their direction and range.

The history of radar

As early as 1904, there were patents for devices to prevent collisions between moving objects. They worked by detecting radio echoes from the objects. However, they could not tell the distances of the objects or their direction of travel.

Early devices transmitted a steady tone of radio waves. Scientists developed pulse transmission in 1925. Measuring the time between transmitting and receiving the pulse could be used to measure the distance of the object from the observer.

Radar development made rapid progress in the 1930s in Europe and the United States. In the United States, scientists at the Naval Research Laboratory discovered that aircraft interfere with radio waves. Later, they incorporated pulse transmission into existing equipment. In the next few years, scientists at the Naval Research Laboratory developed some of the first modern radar equipment.

In Britain, radar research was born out of the prospect of war with Germany. In 1935, Scottish physicist Robert Watson-Watt (1892–1973) invented

◄ *Air traffic controller John J. Jones monitors the AN/SPN-43 Precision Approach Radar from the helicopter direction center during flight operations off the coast of Okinawa, Japan. The AN/SPN-43 is the U.S. Navy's marshaling air traffic control (ATC) radar system used on all aircraft carriers and amphibious assault ships for directing aircraft into a safe landing.*

BLOCK DIAGRAM OF PULSE RADAR

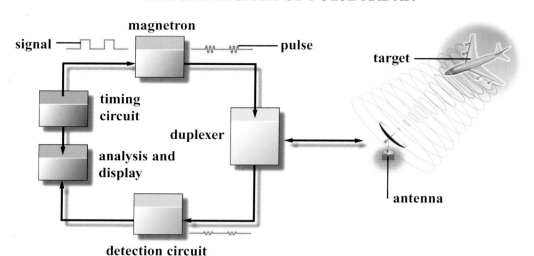

The timing circuit emits electrical pulses at regular intervals. These trigger the magnetron, which produces high-energy radio pulses that are directed to the antenna by a duplexer (a switching circuit). The duplexer directs returning echo signals to the detection circuit between pulses.

radar equipment for the detection of aircraft. By 1938, the British military had built a series of radar stations along the River Thames in London.

Radar devices built on land can be very large, but aircraft-based radar is limited by the size of the airplane. This became important to Britain during World War II (1939–1945). Scientists soon came up with the idea of using microwaves, but there was no equipment that could handle these tiny radio waves. A scientific team began to work with American systems. By 1940, workable equipment had been developed. As a result of the success, American and British scientists often collaborated on radar research. One of their joint inventions was the plan position indicator (PPI)—a radar-display system in which the face of a cathode ray tube is swept by a beam that illuminates it.

During the 1920s, radar research also turned toward the sky. Scientists found out how long it took for radio waves to bounce back to Earth. Knowing the speed at which radio waves travel, it was possible to calculate how far away the ionosphere (reflecting layer of the atmosphere) is from Earth's surface. The same idea was applied to measuring the distance of aircraft, and the use of a directional antenna gave the exact location. This led to the widespread use of radar for air traffic control as well as for air navigation. After making radar contact with Venus in 1958 and the Sun in 1959, astronomers began to use radar regularly in their studies of outer space.

Radar reflections

Similar to visible light, radio waves are a form of electromagnetic radiation and therefore travel at 186,000 miles (300,000 kilometers) per second. By transmitting a radio signal and timing its journey to an object and back to the receiver, the distance of an object can be calculated. This is known as the range. Add details of the direction from which the signal is being reflected—the bearing—and the exact position of the object will be known.

Radio waves are sent out in pulses in a particular direction. Each pulse lasts for a few millionths of a second. The time between each pulse is more than enough for the radio waves to travel to an object and back again.

A single antenna is usually used for transmitting and receiving the signal. The receiver shuts off while the pulse is actually being transmitted and then comes on again to pick up the returned signal. The receiver is operated by a switch called a TR (transmit/receive) cell, which is itself triggered by the transmitter pulse.

Eye on the sky

When searching for an object, or keeping a general lookout, the antenna turns horizontally in a process called scanning. The beam from the antenna is called a fan beam because the area it covers is shaped like an open fan. It is a narrow beam, rising from the horizon by perhaps 15 or 20 degrees.

The basic radar system provides details only of range and bearing. More complex systems can tell the elevation (height) of an object as well. This can be done by various methods. For example, a number of vertical sections of the fan beam can scan at the same time, resulting in a "stack" of beams. In other systems, a narrow pencil beam scans up and down at high speed while being turned horizontally at slow speed.

The direction of an object is normally judged by simply looking for the point at which the reflected signal is strongest. However, the object can be pinpointed even more accurately by making two beams overlap. In the area of overlap, it is possible to figure out the direction of an object very accurately by comparing the two signals. These two beams may be made to spin around the central line of the overlapping area—the equisignal line. This is known as a conical scanning aerial.

An important use of radar is to follow the path of moving objects, for example, airplanes or missiles. This is known as tracking. The tracking beam is usually shaped like a cone or a pencil. As soon as the beam finds the target, it can follow its movements automatically. It is said to be "locked on" to the target.

Transmitting the pulse

Radio pulses beamed out by the radar transmitter must be very powerful. However, the pulses last a short time and are spaced far apart. For example, pulses lasting four microseconds, spaced at periods of four milliseconds, will mean that the transmitter is using power for only one thousandth of the total operating time.

Displays

When the receiver picks up the reflected signals, it amplifies (strengthens) them and displays them on a screen. The shape of the object can be seen fairly clearly on the screen, and its position is known at a glance. The most basic kind of radar display has a cathode ray tube, similar to the one in a television set. The cathode ray beam passes back and forth across the face of the tube at a steady rate. It shows up as a bright spot, tracing a line behind it.

For each radar pulse, the spot moves from left to right. It returns to the left with the start of the next pulse. If the signal is reflected, however, the spot flies back to the left, tracing a line behind it. The length of this line is a measure of the time taken for the reflected pulse to return.

A more normal display screen is called the plan position indicator (PPI). In this device, the tube face shows a maplike view of the area being scanned. The cathode ray beam is adjusted so that a bright "blip" occurs only when something is being reflected. The reflected signals from these transmissions are shown as spots of light. These appear on the radar map in the same place that the distant object would appear on a navigational map. This trace is very faint, and, starting from the center of the tube, goes around and around in time with the scanning aerial.

◄ *This Marconi S500 surveillance radar antenna is used to cover ground-based operations at an airfield in Southend-on-Sea, England.*

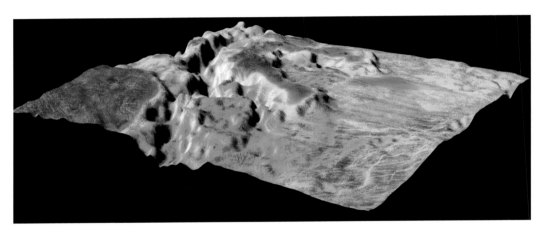

◀ **Radar imaging reveals a topographical map of the surface of Venus. The image was captured during NASA's Magellan orbit of Venus in 1994.**

Doppler radar

When a sound is heard, its pitch will be higher or lower, depending upon whether the source of the sound is moving toward or away from the observer. The Doppler effect also applies to radio waves. Any objects that are not moving, for example, trees or buildings, do not show any change of frequency. However, moving objects, such as planes or rockets, do. In this way, it is possible to show only moving objects on the radar display.

Another use of the Doppler effect is to measure the speed of airplanes. A pilot can use radar to record the echoes from the ground over which he or she is flying. By noting the way in which the frequency of the reflected signal changes, the speed of the airplane can be calculated.

Range and wavelengths

Radar waves travel more or less in a straight line out in space. In Earth's atmosphere, however, a slight bending of the waves takes place. A far bigger problem for the engineer is the curvature of Earth itself. Just as people lose sight of a ship as it disappears over the curve of the horizon, so does radar—it cannot reach far beyond the horizon.

The higher the transmitter, the farther the horizon and range of the radio signal. Many international defense systems now carry radar in airplanes, so that even very low-flying enemy airplanes or missiles will show up on the radar display. For example, an airborne early warning (AEW) system protects both the Atlantic and Pacific coasts of the United States.

All objects can reflect radio waves to some extent. Just how much of a signal they reflect depends on the shape and size of the target and on the wavelength used in the transmission. The first British AEW system used wavelengths of 32 to 50 feet (10 to 15 meters). These wavelengths can detect large objects such as airplanes and ships, but smaller objects show up better with much smaller wavelengths. Most radars now use wavelengths of between 1 and 10 inches (2.5 and 25 centimeters).

Two-way radar

Another form of radar has been developed that makes it possible to identify an airplane. It is called secondary radar, the basic system being known as primary radar. With secondary radar, an airplane carries a small device called a transponder. This is both a receiver and a transmitter. It receives pulses from the ground radar and transmits them back to the ground on a slightly different wavelength. Added to this signal are pulses that make up a special code. The code signal tells the controller on the ground exactly which airplane is on the screen and gives details of its height and position.

Radar has also become important as a remote sensor for scientists. For example, images of northern Africa taken during space shuttle flights, by a radar that "sees" below surfaces, showed river valleys buried under the Sahara desert.

See also: AIRPLANE • AIRPORT • DOPPLER EFFECT • RADIO • SONAR

Radio

Radio is the name given to a system of transmitting and receiving messages through space using electromagnetic radiation called radio waves. Few inventions have changed the lives of people as much as radio. Before radio, news used to travel slowly. Now radio broadcasts help people keep in touch with one another on land and sea, in the air, and even in space.

The first person to send a message using radio waves rather than the telegraph wire was German physicist Heinrich Hertz (1857–1894) around 1886. In honor of his work on radio waves, the word *hertz* is used as the unit of frequency of such waves. Hertz was not especially interested in sending speech over the air. This idea was taken up by Italian physicist and inventor Guglielmo Marconi (1874–1937), who began his work about eight years after Hertz's first transmission.

By the time Marconi became interested in what was then called wireless telegraphy, there had been important laboratory experiments by English physicist Oliver Lodge (1851–1940) and Russian physicist and electrical engineer Alexsandr Popov (1859–1905). French physicist Édouard-Eugéne Branly (1844–1940) had also invented a simple radio detector. Building on these foundations, Marconi invented the wireless receiver of radio waves and patented it in England in 1896.

In 1897, Marconi set up the Wireless Telegraph Company Limited in London, England, to transmit long-distance messages by radio waves instead of by electrical signals. A year later, he sent a radio message across the English Channel between England and France. In 1901, Marconi then succeeded in receiving and sending signals across the Atlantic Ocean between Poldhu in Cornwall, England, and St. John's, Newfoundland.

▲ *Communications towers such as these broadcast radio transmissions over hundreds of miles.*

In 1906, the first radio broadcasts were made in the United States and Germany, but little attention was paid to them. Early radio receivers were difficult to use, and the sound that came from them was not particularly good. Later, the crystal (magnetite or silicon) radio receiver improved the sound for the listener. Speech and music were reproduced with improved quality with the

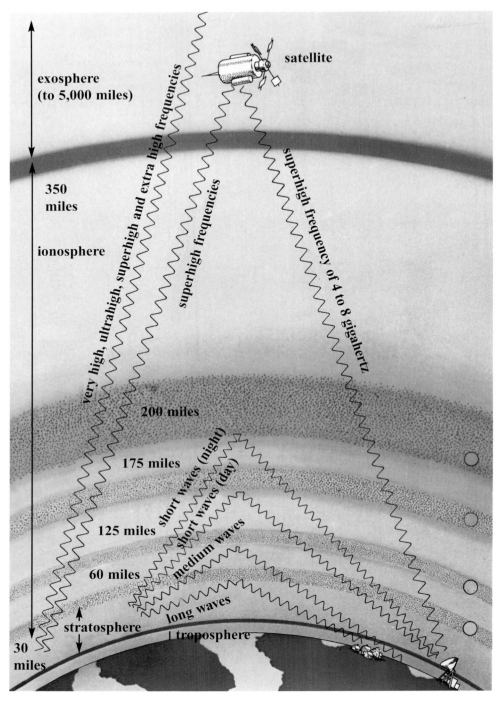

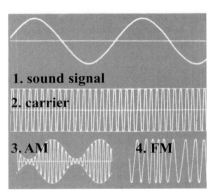

▲ The sound signal (1) is carried by the carrier wave (2). The sound signal is used to modulate (vary) the wave in some way. Amplitude modulation (AM; 3) and frequency modulation (FM; 4) are both used for general broadcasting.

◄ The atmosphere surrounding Earth can be divided into sections. The inner layer is called the troposphere, and the middle layer is called the stratosphere. The outer layers are known as the ionosphere and exosphere and consist of charged particles. These layers reflect some radio waves, so that they can be picked up over a wider area. However, high frequency microwaves pass through the particles of the ionosphere. This makes it possible for them to be used in satellite communications, which play an important part in radio broadcasting.

invention of the "Audion" triode vacuum tube by U.S. inventor Lee De Forest (1873–1961). In 1912, U.S. electrical engineer Edwin H. Armstrong (1890–1954) made possible long-range broadcasting following his discovery of the feedback, or regenerative, circuit. In 1933, Armstrong developed the frequency modulation (FM) system of radio, which is still in use.

However, it was almost by accident that radio grew into the large entertainment industry that it has become. Amateur radio operators, nicknamed hams, began to play music and tell jokes. The idea caught on. In 1920, the first regular radio station— Station KDKA in Pittsburgh—broadcast the results of the presidential election, in which Warren Harding triumphed over James Cox.

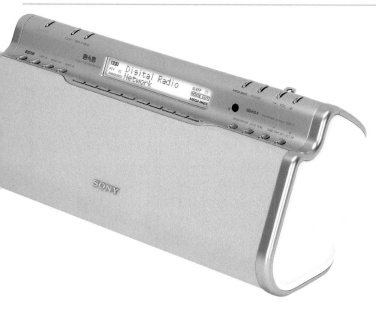

▲ *Digital radios offer more choice, improved sound quality, and extra information on broadcasts. This particular Sony model has an optical digital output to enable digital recordings to a minidisc or CD player.*

Domestic radio sets were not easy to use during the 1920s. The first loudspeaker was simply a headphone, with cone-shaped devices called megaphones attached to increase the volume. So little power was used to send radio waves that the sound could be heard only in a quiet room.

By the 1930s, the sending and receiving of radio broadcasts had improved, and radio entertainment had become popular. Radio sets soon became part of every household.

What are radio waves?

Radio waves are a form of electromagnetic radiation consisting of a combination of electric and magnetic fields. Radio waves travel at the same speed as light—approximately 186,000 miles (300,000 kilometers) per second. The peaks of the waves are the points at which the electric and magnetic fields are at their greatest.

The frequency of a radio wave is the number of times per second that these fields peak in one direction, peak in the other direction, and return to the original peak. The wavelength is the distance between two peaks in the same direction. The higher the frequency of a radio wave, the shorter the wavelength.

How does radio transmission work?

The heart of any radio transmitter is an electrical circuit called an oscillator, which produces an alternating voltage (carrier wave) at the frequency to be used for transmission. This signal must be modified in some way to carry information or sound. The simplest method of transmitting information involved interrupting the signal using a simple switch or key to form the long and short dashes and dots of Morse code. To transmit speech or music, however, a more rapid modification, called modulation, of the signal must be achieved.

There are two forms of modulation in current use. In amplitude modulation (AM), the amplitude (strength) of the sine wave generated by the oscillator is made to vary in time to match the intensity of the sound wave (audio) signal received from a microphone. In frequency modulation (FM), the frequency of the signal is varied in time by a small amount proportional to the strength of the audio signal being transmitted.

Once the signal is modulated, it is amplified, or made larger in voltage, by additional signals so that a powerful version of the original modulated signal is applied to the antenna. The antenna consists of two electrical conductors along which electrons move at the frequency of the applied signal, producing the electromagnetic wave. Sometimes, the ground (earth) is used as one of the conductors.

How does radio reception work?

Each radio receiver has an antenna. Each passing electromagnetic wave induces a small time-varying voltage in the antenna. The antenna is connected to a tuning circuit, which eliminates voltages except those near the frequency selected by the listener. The remaining signal is then sent onto an amplifier and demodulator, which extract the audio signal from the rapidly varying carrier signal and permit it to be heard over a loudspeaker or headphones.

AM radio

Some radios receive three bands—short wave, medium wave, and long wave—for AM broadcasts. For an AM transmitter to work well, the carrier

Jerry Springer at the controls in a studio from where his new radio show for the Capital Gold station will be broadcast in London, England.

frequency must be steady. If it is not, the reception will be poor and will likely fade. This problem is solved by the use of a crystal oscillator that keeps the frequency steady. The crystals are usually made of quartz, which is very reliable. The voltage output from the crystal oscillator is called a sine wave. It is raised to a high power level by a series of radio frequency amplifiers. This forms the carrier wave.

The signal is first strengthened with a low-frequency amplifier. Then it is passed to a modulating amplifier. In this way, the carrier wave can be modulated according to the strength of the signal at any one time. For the best transmission, it is necessary to make an efficient transfer of power to the antenna. This can be done only if the impedance (apparent resistance) of the output is the same as the impedance of the antenna. This task is carried out by a matching network.

The carrier waves are transmitted from the antenna. Radio waves travel outward from a simple, straight-wire antenna in the same way as ripples on water spread out in circles when a pebble is thrown into a pond. More complex antennas make it possible for waves to be directed or beamed.

The receiver antenna works like the transmitter antenna, only in reverse. It also makes use of matching networks to get the best possible transfer of power from the antenna to the input circuitry.

When a radio set is tuned to a particular station, it will accept only the carrier frequency of that particular transmitter. In its simplest form, the tuning circuit consists of a coil and a capacitor. This resonant circuit has a resonant frequency that can be adjusted by the variable capacitor until it matches the frequency of the transmitter.

Having passed through an amplifier, the signal is demodulated (unscrambled from the carrier wave). The signal is then passed through a low-frequency amplifier and loudspeaker, emerging as the evening news or your favorite music station.

FM radio

Other radio signals, interference from electrical machinery, and even thunderstorms can affect AM transmission. This problem of noise was solved by frequency modulation (FM), which offers a better reception. However, it does need a much larger frequency band width than AM. FM is used widely in very-high frequency (VHF) and ultrahigh frequency (UHF) broadcasting.

Who broadcasts where?

The wavelengths of all radio stations are prescribed by the International Telecommunications Union. Some bands are reserved for special uses. VHF and UHF frequencies are used by airplanes, ships, the military, the police, and other two-way operators. The lower end of the long-wave band is used for marine communications and navigation.

Digital radio

Digital radio is a new way of broadcasting radio using the same technology as computers and compact discs (CDs). Digital radio provides a better reception and higher-quality sound than current AM and FM radio broadcasts. One main difference is that digital radio involves the delivery of digital signals that can be used not only for sound broadcasting, but also multimedia services.

See also: ANTENNA • BROADCASTING • MICROWAVE RADIATION • RADAR

Radioactivity

Some chemical elements give off energy by changing their internal structure. This energy is called radiation, and the element is said to be going through radioactive decay. Radioactive substances are used in many industrial processes, and to fight cancer, to help diagnose diseases, to kill bacteria, and to sterilize food and drugs.

Radioactivity was discovered in 1896 by French physicist Antoine-Henri Becquerel (1852–1908). Becquerel was experimenting with uranium salts that could fluoresce (glow). Becquerel wanted to see if they were emitting (giving off) X-rays. Only the year before, German physicist Wilhelm Röntgen (1845–1923) had discovered that X-rays could make a glass tube fluoresce.

Becquerel took a photographic plate and wrapped it in black paper to protect it from light. He then put a silver coin on top of the plate and a crystal of a uranium compound on top of the coin.

Becquerel left the plate for a few days and then carefully developed it. He was delighted to find that the plate was black all over except for the part covered by the silver coin. He realized that the uranium salt must be emitting some sort of radiation that had penetrated the paper and affected the emulsion on the photographic plate. Becquerel decided that the rays coming out of the uranium were not like X-rays because they were being emitted on their own.

Becquerel's discovery was the first work done on radioactivity. His revolutionary discovery was continued by other scientists, including Polish chemist Marie Curie (1867–1934) and French chemist Pierre Curie (1859–1906), who discovered the chemical elements polonium and radium. These had not been detected before because they are so rare. All these new elements are unstable (unsettled) and emit very penetrating radiation. As they emit the radiation, they change into different elements. This transformation had never been seen before and was called *radioactivity*—a term coined by Marie Curie. The process that causes the elements to change is called radioactive decay.

◄ *A scientist uses a mass spectrometer in carbon dating. The spectrometer is used to analyze the amount of carbon-12 in carbon dioxide, produced by the combustion of the sample in oxygen. The carbon-14 content of the sample is assessed using a linear accelerator. The ratio of radioactive carbon-14 to stable carbon-12 can be used to figure out the age of the sample being investigated.*

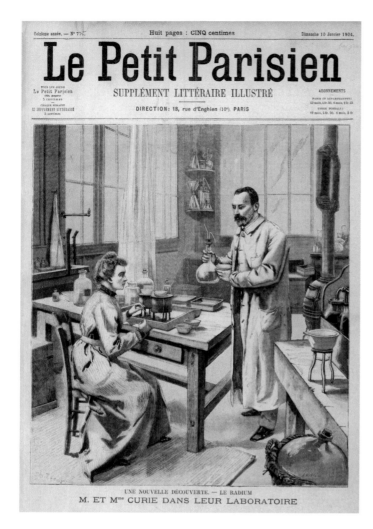

Le Petit Parisien
SUPPLÉMENT LITTÉRAIRE ILLUSTRÉ

UNE NOUVELLE DÉCOUVERTE. — LE RADIUM
M. ET Mme CURIE DANS LEUR LABORATOIRE

▲ *This illustration of scientists Marie and Pierre Curie in their laboratory appeared on the front page of the journal* **Le Petit Parisien** *on January 10, 1904. Marie Curie won the 1911 Nobel Prize for chemistry for her discovery of the radioactive elements polonium and radium.*

Inside the atom

Becquerel's experiment showed that the atoms consist of even smaller particles. A radioactive atom is losing something—it is breaking down. Scientists now know that it is the dense nucleus at the center of the atom that emits particles or rays. What is also interesting about radioactive decay is that it is not affected by any chemical reaction or by doing anything to the nucleus.

The nuclei of most atoms consist of two kinds of particles: positively charged protons and uncharged neutrons. The number of protons in the nucleus determines the number of electrons needed for electrical neutrality and thus the chemical properties of the atom. Neutrons are electrically neutral and thus have no effect on the chemical properties of the atom.

Half-life

If there are too many or too few neutrons in the nucleus, the nucleus is unstable, and it will change by radioactive decay until it becomes stable. The time it takes to decay is measured by the half-life of the material. The half-life is the time taken for half the number of atoms present at the start to have decayed. Some half-lives are as short as a fraction of a second. Others are as long as millions of years.

Alpha decay

There are several different ways in which a radioactive atom can decay. One is by alpha decay. Sometimes, when a nucleus is too heavy to be stable, it throws out two protons and two neutrons. This arrangement is similar to the nucleus of a helium atom. When this type of decay was first discovered in helium, the nuclei were called alpha particles. Alpha decay is very common among the heavier elements, such as radium and uranium.

Alpha particles are energetic particles, but they are bulky. So they can pass through only about 1 inch (2.5 centimeters) of air and will not penetrate human skin. If they enter a person's body by accident through a wound or as dust in the air, they can do a lot of damage because the outer skin will stop them from leaving the body.

Elements that emit alpha particles naturally are not often used now that artificial radioactive isotopes are available. However, uranium and plutonium both give off alpha particles and are important in the nuclear power industry.

Beta decay

When a nucleus has too many neutrons, one neutron can change into a proton and electron. The electron is then ejected from the nucleus as a beta particle, which can travel several yards through air, through a few inches of tissue, or through ⅛ inch

(3 millimeters) of metal or plastic. Beta particles can burn painfully if they touch the skin. If they get inside a person's body, they will do great harm.

Beta decay is the most common type of radioactive decay among artificial isotopes. Strontium-90 is a good source of beta particles. Such substances are called radioisotopes.

Some artificial radioisotopes have too few neutrons rather than too many. They decay by emitting positrons, which are positively charged electrons. These interact almost immediately with ordinary electrons. Such isotopes are often used to diagnose illnesses.

Gamma ray emission

Gamma rays are produced when beta decay has taken place in a nucleus, but the nucleus has not become stable. Similar to visible light and X-rays, gamma rays are electromagnetic radiation. Cobalt-60 is a good source of gamma rays.

Using artificial radioisotopes

Various artificial radioisotopes are manufactured for many different purposes. They can be used to detect forgeries of art and also in agriculture, industry, and medicine.

In the past, people have copied paintings by famous artists and have sold them for vast sums of money. It is now possible to test paintings using radioisotopes to see whether or not they are fakes. A tiny sample of the painting is taken. A stream of neutrons is then showered onto the sample, and this makes the sample radioactive. From the

radiation emitted, it is possible to tell the age of the painting and the type of paints used. This process is called neutron activation analysis.

In industry, several artificial radioisotopes are used to reveal defects in materials and also to check their thicknesses. In medicine, artificial radioisotopes are used for radioactive scanning of a person's body. This gives a picture of parts of the body that cannot be reached by X-rays. The doses used must be small so that they will not harm the person. Larger doses of substances such as cobalt-60 are used to kill cancers, but they may also cause cancer themselves.

Telling time with carbon-14

Carbon is present in all living things. Plants take in carbon in the form of carbon dioxide, animals then eat the plants, and people eat plants and animals.

One isotope of carbon is radioactive. It is called carbon-14. Carbon-14 is made in the top part of the atmosphere above Earth. It is produced when neutrons from cosmic rays react with atoms of nitrogen. Carbon dioxide in the air always contains some carbon-14.

As soon as a plant dies, it stops taking in carbon dioxide, and therefore it stops taking in any more carbon-14. The carbon-14 emits beta particles and decays with a half-life of about 5,730 years. The rate at which the atoms of carbon-14 decay is measured by the number of disintegrations per minute. Just 0.03 ounces (1 gram) of carbon-14 decays at a rate of 15 disintegrations a minute. So 5,730 years after the plant has died, the count rate will have dropped to 7½ disintegrations a minute. It is therefore possible to tell when the plant died by measuring the count rate. This process is called carbon dating.

Carbon dating has been used to date Egyptian tombs, the Dead Sea Scrolls, Stonehenge (a ring of giant stones in Britain), and some materials that have been shown to be more than 20,000 years old.

See also: ATOM AND MOLECULE • CARBON DATING • CURIE, MARIE AND PIERRE • MEDICAL TECHNOLOGY • NUCLEAR REACTOR

Radiotherapy

Radiation therapy, or radiotherapy, is a medical technique that uses radiation to control the growth and spread of cancer cells in the body. X-rays and gamma rays have a lot of energy, and it is this energy that is used to destroy the cancer cells. Radiation can also destroy healthy cells, so radiotherapy has to be used with care.

Radiotherapy uses X-rays and gamma radiation. Both are forms of electromagnetic radiation similar to microwaves, radio waves, and sunlight. It is the high energy of X-rays and gamma radiation that can be used in radiotherapy to control or destroy abnormal body cells such as cancer cells.

Gamma rays are produced naturally by elements such as cesium and cobalt. X-rays have to be produced artificially, by bombarding tungsten with electricity. X-rays are used for many forms of radiotherapy, but for deep-lying tumors needing high-energy radiation, gamma rays are more often used. A gamma-ray unit is a quantity of radioactive cesium or cobalt inside a thick lead casing. During treatment, a small hole is opened in the casing to allow the gamma rays out.

How does radiotherapy work?

X-rays and gamma rays damage all living cells, but cells that are growing or dividing are damaged more easily than others. Cancer cells grow and divide very rapidly compared to healthy cells, so radiotherapy affects them far more than normal cells. Radiotherapy also destroys the small blood vessels that nourish cancer cells.

How is radiotherapy used?

Cancer cells can grow and cause tumors in all parts of the body. Different types of radiotherapy have to be used for different tumors. If a skin tumor needs treatment, then low-energy radiation can be used. If a tumor in the lung is to be treated, however, then a powerful X-ray machine has to be used so that the radiation can penetrate deep inside the body.

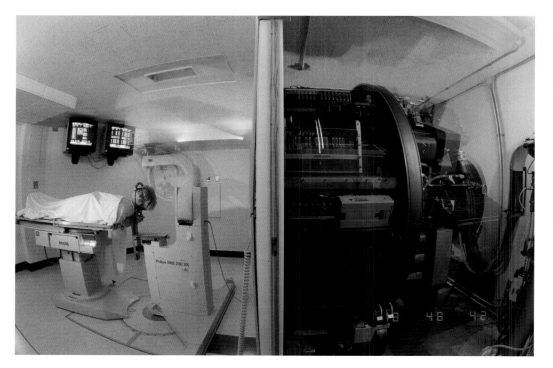

◄ A woman lies beneath a lead-lined sheet with her head stabilized by a steel frame. Behind the wall, a linear accelerator fires radiation at a tumor in the woman's brain. The linear accelerator allows the physician to pinpoint radiation to the precise location of the tumor, sparing the surrounding normal tissue and organs.

Powerful radiation does not differentiate between healthy cells and abnormal cancer cells, so it is important that the beam of X-rays or gamma rays is carefully directed. The narrowest possible radiation beam is used, and the healthy areas are protected with lead shielding.

Some tumors may be treated by placing a substance that will give off radiation in the body, close to the tumor. Needles, tubes, wires, or pellets containing radioactive material are placed in the body next to or even in the tumor. These radioactive materials produce only low-energy radiation so that healthy tissues are not damaged.

Radiotherapy treatment

When using radiotherapy, the exact location of the tumor must be found through medical-imaging techniques such as magnetic resonance imaging (MRI), positron emission tomography (PET), and X-ray imaging. Computers are now generally used to calculate the energy, size, and position of the radiation beam. The beam positions are then marked on the patient's skin to ensure that he or she is in exactly the right position for each treatment.

During the procedure, the patient sits or lies beneath the radiation beam for a few minutes. The treatment itself is quite painless. It takes place in a room shielded with lead and concrete so that no harmful radiation affects anyone else. The course of treatment is usually spread over a few weeks and is divided into three to five doses each week. Dividing the doses allows for better recovery of the body's healthy cells and increases the total radiation dose directed at the tumor.

Side effects

The side effects of radiotherapy can be immediate or delayed. Most patients experience some short-term side effects, including fatigue, loss of appetite, and soreness of the skin at the site of the treatment. If the scalp is involved, some hair may fall out, but this usually grows back. If the intestines, mouth, or stomach are involved, the patient may feel nauseous or have diarrhea, but this can be controlled with drugs. Long-term side effects occur in only a small

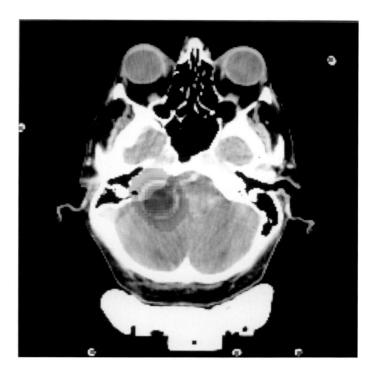

▲ **A three-dimensional computer-generated image reveals the location of a brain tumor (in red). Medical imaging allows the precise mapping of once inoperable brain tumors, enabling the precise delivery of intense radiotherapy to fight the tumor.**

number of patients. Infertility may result in cases of treatment to the ovaries or testes. Radiotherapy involving treatment of brain tumors may cause memory problems and personality changes. However, in these cases it is often difficult to tell if the symptoms are side effects of radiotherapy or are caused by the resurgence of a tumor.

Results of radiotherapy

Most cancers are easily destroyed by radiotherapy, and the tumors usually disappear completely. Other tumors are harder to treat, especially those lying deep inside the body. Many tumors are removed by surgery, and then radiotherapy is used just in case any cancer cells have been left behind. With other cancers, radiation is used successfully to treat and control the tumors as they are found.

See also: CELL • DISEASE • MEDICAL IMAGING • MEDICAL TECHNOLOGY • RADIOACTIVITY

Glossary

Alloys Mixtures of metals with other elements, often other metals or carbon, to make them stronger or give them certain qualities.

Alternating current (AC) An electrical current that reverses periodically. Domestic electricity supplies use alternating current.

Alternator A type of generator that produces an alternating electrical current.

Amino acids Organic molecules consisting of a central carbon atom, a carboxyl group (–COOH), and a side chain (–R). Amino acids are the building blocks of proteins.

Amplitude modulation (AM) A radio broadcasting technique in which the radio signal is always of the same frequency, but its amplitude varies.

Catalysts Substances that initiate or speed up chemical reactions without themselves being used up during the reaction.

Cavitation The process by which an object is worn away by bubbles created as the object moves through a liquid, such as a ship's propeller through water.

Direct current (DC) An electrical current that flows continuously in one direction. The current from a battery is an example of direct current.

Emulsion A mixture of two or more liquids in which one liquid is present as droplets of microscopic size distributed throughout the other.

Enzymes Proteins that catalyze chemical reactions in biological systems.

Eukaryotes Organisms composed of one or more cells containing distinct nuclei and organelles.

Eutrophication Rapid increase in the nutrients contained in a body of water; it may occur naturally or as a consequence of human activities, such as the overuse of fertilizers in agriculture.

Extrusion A molding process whereby a viscous molten substance is forced through a small hole.

Fetus Unborn offspring after it has completed most of its development; in humans, the term applies from the second or third month of pregnancy to birth.

Frequency modulation (FM) A radio broadcasting technique for improving the quality of sound in which the radio signal is always the same strength but comes at varying times per second.

Friction The resistance encountered when one body is moved in contact with another.

Hormones Chemicals secreted into the blood by ductless glands and carried to specific cells, organs, or tissues to stimulate chemical activity.

Isotope Any of two or more forms of a chemical element with the same atomic number but different nuclear masses.

Lithosphere Outer layer of Earth, composed of hard, rigid crustal rocks.

Photoelectric effect Emission of electrons from the surface of a metal when the metal is hit by electromagnetic radiation at certain frequencies.

Plasma One of the four states of matter, plasma is a collection of charged particles in which the numbers of positive and negative ions are approximately equal.

Polarization In optics, the process of reducing the glare of ordinary light by making the light waves vibrate in one direction only and filtering out the unwanted light.

Polymer Molecule that consists of simple, repeating units called monomers.

Prokaryotes Typically single-celled organisms that lack distinct nuclei and organelles.

Pseudopod An extension of an amoeboid cell that is used for feeding and locomotion.

Radiation Energy radiated or transmitted as rays, waves, or in the form of particles. Visible light and X-rays are examples of radiation.

Sublimation The conversion of a solid into a gas or a gas into a solid without becoming a liquid.

Transformer A device that steps up (increases) or steps down (decreases) an electrical force.

Vacuum A space entirely devoid of matter, or more generally, a space that has been exhausted to a high degree by an air pump or other artificial means.

Index

Page numbers in **bold** refer to main articles; those in *italics* refer to illustrations.